My Heart's at Home

Jill Savage

HARVEST HOUSE PUBLISHERS

EUGENE, OREGON

Cover by Garborg Design Works, Savage, Minnesota

Cover photo © Time and Again, Reed Family Photography, East Peoria, IL October, 2006

Published in association with the literary agency of Alive Communications, Inc., 7680 Goddard Street, Ste #200, Colorado Springs, CO 80920

Harvest House Publishers has made every effort to trace the ownership of all quotes. In the event of a question arising from the use of a quote, we regret any error made and will be pleased to make the necessary correction in future editions of this book.

MY HEART'S AT HOME
Copyright © 2007 by Jill Savage
Published by Harvest House Publishers
Eugene, Oregon 97402
www.harvesthousepublishers.com

Library of Congress Cataloging-in-Publication Data
Savage, Jill, 1964-
My heart's at home / Jill Savage.
p. cm.
ISBN-13: 978-0-7369-1826-8 (pbk.)
ISBN-10: 0-7369-1826-4 (pbk.)
1. Home—Religious aspects—Christianity. I. Title.
BR115.H56S28 2007
248.4—dc22

2006021483

Printed in the United States of America

08 09 10 11 12 13 14 15 / VP-SK / 10 9 8 7 6 5 4 3

Kristin Jukes

~ Contents ~

What Is a Home?

What do you think of when you hear the word home?
What images and emotions come to mind? This is something
to ponder, for these images and emotions have the power to
shape your life, to give it meaning, to tell you who you are.

THOMAS KINKADE

My husband, Mark, and I walked through the well-lived-in farmhouse marveling at the size of the rooms. There was a lot of space: large kitchen and dining room, good-sized family room and living room, one bedroom for an office, a small bathroom—and that was just on the main floor.

Upstairs were five bedrooms! Yep, five bedrooms…and no bathroom. One small bathroom on the main floor for our family of six? Well, of course this house needed some work. What farmhouse wouldn't? And what would it take to add a bathroom upstairs? No problem. But that wasn't all. It was not only a perfect house, but it was in a perfect location: smack-dab in the middle of cornfields and yet only two and a half miles from Wal-Mart. What more could we want? Our dream to live in the country was going to finally come true.

We made several trips to look at this house with our Realtor. On the final trip, we were determining what we were going to offer the seller when another Realtor and interested party stopped by. They asked if we minded if they took a quick tour of the home, even though we were present. We told them to go right ahead. As the Realtor's client stepped through the entryway into the kitchen,

he said, "This place is a pit. I don't want to see any more." They
walked out of the house and then Mark and I looked at each other
and laughed. We didn't see the liabilities of this old farmhouse—we
saw its possibilities!

We signed the papers and, with the help of friends and family, set
to work, determining to do most of the renovation before we moved
in. Our four children ranged from ages twelve to nine months.
We decided the best strategy was for Mark to work evenings and
weekends at the house and I would get a sitter occasionally so I
could help him, but ultimately I prepared myself for full kid duty
twenty-four hours a day for however long this took.

It took four months.

We tore out all of the carpet because the entire house needed new
floor coverings. We uncovered pocket doors that had been closed
off years ago. We painted woodwork that was already painted and
cleaned and stained woodwork that was still in its natural state.
We washed and painted every wall and ceiling. We tore out the
plumbing for the only bathroom because the floor had rotted and
we feared someone might just sit on the pot one day and fall through
to the cellar.

But that wasn't all. We still had the "no bathroom on the second
floor" problem, so we made a decision to tear off the entryway and a
small enclosed porch, pour a new foundation, and add a two-story
addition: a small room and an entryway on the main floor and a
laundry room and a bathroom on the second floor. We also decided
that because there was no garage, we would add an attached garage
off the back of the house.

We didn't hire anyone to do the construction work—we did it all
ourselves with the exception of hiring an electrician and contracting
someone to pour the foundation.

It was a lot of work.

I often think back to that time in our life nearly ten years ago.
We had a dream *and* we had the vision to see the dream come true.
When we looked at the house, we didn't see it for what it was. We
saw it for what it would become.

There was another construction project we were managing even while constructing and reconstructing our new home: We were building a family. We had a dream and the vision to see that dream come true as well.

Many of the home-building experiences we've had with our farmhouse have mirrored the experiences we've had building our family. Sometimes we've had to tear down an old structure that we carried with us from our families of origin and build something new and different. Sometimes we've had to start from scratch and build a completely new structure within our family because we have a vision for something different than either of us have ever known. In both cases we've had a plan, and we've carried out that plan with intentionality.

When we renovated, we drew up blueprints to help us visualize the new part of our home. Seeing the details on paper kept us on track and working toward the same goals. In the same way, we've needed a blueprint for our family. Similar to the steps in building a home, there are foundational elements we need to have in place so we can build a strong family structure. Once the foundation is poured, we begin to build the framework, and eventually we put on the finishing details.

But what makes a house a home? It's the family dynamics of the people who live in that house that makes it a home. When we value being home and recognize all the roles that home plays in our life, we can provide a secure, loving environment for each member of our family.

Home—there's a warmth about that word. It's associated with love and security. It's a place where we are known, accepted, and celebrated. But a house isn't what we are really drawn to—it's the memories, the feelings we experience that draw us home. And a house can't provide memories itself—it's the people, the family that draws our heart to home.

Our neighborhoods are filled with broken hearts and broken homes. Many of us came from broken homes and broken families, longing for something different for our own family but not quite knowing how to get there. We know home is important because we can identify the qualities that we experienced or longed for as a child. Now that we have our own families, we need a blueprint to help us build and/or renovate our home and family.

My Heart's at Home is designed to help us understand all the roles that home plays in our life:

Home as…a safe house
   …a rest area
      …a trauma unit
         …a church

Home as…a pep rally
   …a research lab
      …a school
         …a museum

Home as…a playground
   …a business office
      …a hospitality house
         …a cultural center

Home is central to understanding who we are, who we belong to, and what we stand for. It is hope, promise, and love. Home isn't about the structure we live in; it's about our connection to the people who live in the structure with us.

In this book you'll learn a lot about the people who live in my home, so I believe introductions are in order. My husband, Mark, and I have been married 23 years, 13 of them happily. We're a living example that two people can restore love to what eventually became a loveless marriage. Most of that story is found in my book *Is There Really Sex After Kids?* (Zondervan), but you'll hear snippets of it in this book as well. Our oldest daughter, Anne, is 22 years old. She's been married less than a year to Matt, the son-in-law we prayed for all of Anne's life. Our oldest son, Evan, is 19 and a sophomore in college. He's studying music business and hopes to someday make a living with his musical talents. Erica is 16 years old and a sophomore in high school. She loves musical theater and fashion design. Kolya is the newest member to our family. He's 13 years old, but has only been a "Savage" for three and a half years. We adopted Kolya from Russia at the age of nine. However, you'd hardly know that now, as his transition into our family has been very smooth. Austin is our youngest. He's ten years old and in the fifth grade. Both Kolya and Austin love sports, and they are both learning to play an instrument in the school band (earplugs, anyone?).

I've been at home now for 20 years, and I consider motherhood my profession. I have a college degree (music education), and initially felt I was wasting my education, talents, and skills by being "just a mom." In time, however, my perspective changed, and I began to think of motherhood as a valid career choice. Once I thought of it as a profession, I pursued it with as much intentionality as I would any other career. Eventually I launched Hearts at Home (www.hearts-at-home.org), an organization designed to encourage, educate, and equip women in the profession of motherhood. This book is a Hearts at Home resource, one of many resources available to encourage women to mother with intentionality.

As you turn the following pages, you'll find vision to keep you focused for the long haul of parenting. You'll find encouragement that will keep you going every day. And you'll find perspective that will reframe your understanding of home and empower you to make a home for your family in more ways than you may have ever considered.

PART I
The Foundation

Home as a Safe House

*The happiest moments of my life have been the few which
I have passed at home in the bosom of my family.*

THOMAS JEFFERSON

It was a hot summer day. We had torn off the enclosed patio and a small entryway into our farmhouse. Today was the day we turned the corner from demolition to construction. We were pouring the foundation of an addition on our "new home." This foundation would support a two-story addition that would include a bathroom and laundry room on the second floor.

The foundation of a house determines how safe and secure the building will be. While the foundation isn't usually seen, it's the most important part of the house because everything else is built on top of it. Families are built the same way. The foundational elements of a family lay the groundwork for a positive, loving family environment. We may have a vision for the family and home life we dream of creating, but if we don't pay attention to the foundational elements that will support that dream, we'll find ourselves with a family environment that doesn't feel safe, isn't a refuge from the crazy world we live in, doesn't provide hope when life feels hopeless, and doesn't give us a place to heal from life's hurts. When we recognize the need for home to be a safe house, a place of restoration, a faith environment, and even a trauma unit, we are on our way to creating a firm foundation for a home environment that nurtures, loves, and encourages one another.

Let's begin to explore the foundational elements that turn a house into a home by first understanding the role of home as a safe house.

The Role of a Safe House

They say the house down the street from us was once a part of the Underground Railroad. It stands by itself like a ship amidst a sea of corn and soybean fields. Every time I drive by it, I try to imagine what it would have been like to move from one safe house to the next. I can almost feel the fear that would grip a heart moving from one unknown to another. Once an escaped slave had arrived and was welcomed and well hidden by the "conductor," there had to be a sigh of relief and, for a brief moment, a sense of safety.

A safe house provides protection from the world in which it exists. It recognizes the dangers that lurk in every direction, shielding its inhabitants from their threatening surroundings. When home is a safe house, it provides a foundation of safety in family relationships. This safety is what is needed for us to securely and intimately attach to those closest to us. Let's take a look at what is required to construct a home that is emotionally safe.

Require Respect

Respect is the cornerstone of a safe family. When our thoughts, feelings, and emotions are respected, we feel secure. When our property, privacy, and individuality are respected, we feel protected. Respect speaks value, esteem, admiration, and appreciation.

If respect is so important, how is it that we so easily become disrespectful at home? Why do we treat the ones we love the most with such disdain? Often we show more respect to complete strangers than we do to our own family. This happens because home is where we let down the walls. It's a place where we feel we don't always have to be on our best behavior. And we don't. If home is going to be a safe place, it needs to be a safe place when we're on our best behavior and when we're not. However, sometimes we confuse being in a "safe" environment as having a license for disrespect.

That's when the pendulum swings too far, and we need to bring it back in balance.

Even in the early years of parenting we can establish respect. It starts with respecting other children's toys by teaching respect for property. If you go to someone's home and your toddler plays with their toys, require them to help pick up and put them away when you are ready to leave. When you are walking on a sidewalk and your preschooler wants to take off across the grass on someone's lawn, draw him or her back to the sidewalk and gently explain about respect for property. When your child needs to talk to you and you are in the bathroom or bedroom with the door closed, teach them to knock and share with them about respect for privacy. When you are in a crowded bus or train, talk to your child about respect for age, requiring that they give up their seat for someone older. These are foundational lessons for a lifetime of respect.

What about at home? At home, require respect. Establish a core value of respect within the family, and if that core value is disregarded, address the infringement immediately. In other words, discipline for disrespect.

My parents used to say, "If you can't say something nice, don't say anything at all." Mark and I took that one step further. If a child was being disrespectful to a sibling or us, they lost their freedom of speech. Removing the privilege of speaking is one way to address disrespect within a family. Maybe one child is having trouble with his tongue while in the car on the way home from school. After asking the child if what he said was respectful and his admittance that it wasn't, a simple parental response is "Since you misused your mouth, you have lost your freedom to speak until we get home. After we get home, you'll need to go straight to your bedroom to think about the weight of your words. Then you'll need to make it right with your sister ('I'm sorry. Will you please forgive me?') before you have your freedom restored."

In many families brothers and sisters are downright mean to one another. In a home that requires respect, disrespect simply can't be tolerated. Don't threaten to do something when your offspring say something mean to one another or to you; nip it in the bud right away. Don't simply say, "Don't talk to your brother like that." Let them know their behavior is unacceptable and give a consequence immediately. Dealing with this matter from day one lets them know you are serious.

If your kids are older and you have allowed disrespect, it's not too late to address it. Call a family meeting and explain that from this day forward this will be a home of respect, and if something mean is said to another, a consequence will be experienced (loss of privilege, loss of screens—TV, computer, video games, etc.). Establish the foundation of respect and then protect it fiercely.

Practice Grace and Forgiveness

There is nothing better in this world than to be celebrated for who you are. The natural place for that to happen is within the family unit. However, when you live closely with other people, it becomes easy to criticize each other's shortcomings rather than celebrate the differences. Introducing the concept of forgiveness and grace as well as healthy conflict resolution skills will help family members know how to manage the daily ups and downs of relationships.

Before we can teach our kids about it, we have to understand it for ourselves. I explored the concept of grace in my *Professionalizing Motherhood* book, so I'll simply include an overview of the concept here. Extending grace to someone is allowing them to be human. A family with grace in place allows a family member to make mistakes without being raked over the coals for their blunder. When God extends His grace to us, it means that there is nothing we can do that would cause Him to love us more and there is nothing we can do to cause Him to love us less. Can we say that experience happens in our family? When your husband fails to do what he said he would do, do you turn cold and angry or do you forgive him in your heart and extend grace? Or when your child spills milk on your freshly mopped floor, do you lash out in anger or do you make a better choice by extending grace? After all, we all make mistakes, right?

Most of the time when family members disappoint us, they mess with our sense of justice. We feel the need to let them know that their mistake made life unfair for us or affected us in some way. We feel the need to punish those who do wrong. But God doesn't work that way. When we deserve punishment He gives mercy instead, and that's what's called grace. However, the pathway to grace requires a stop at forgiveness.

Forgiveness is the choice to let go of the hurt. It's a decision to let God handle the justice part of the equation. Forgiveness is life-giving to relationships and freeing to the soul. When you and I choose to live lives of grace, forgiveness is what gets us there. So when your husband fails to do what he said he would do, you are facing a very important Y in the road. You can get angry and lash out at him with condemning, wounding words, or you can have a conversation with God that goes something like this: "God, I do love that man, but right now I don't like him. He disappointed me, and his irresponsibility now has ramifications for me. As hard as it is, though, I choose to forgive him for what happened today." Whew! That's a hard conversation to have with God, but if you and I will learn to have more of those conversations, we will pave the way for loving, grace-filled relationships.

"If I have that kind of conversation with God, does it mean I can't talk to my husband about how his actions affected me?" you might ask. The answer is, "Absolutely not!" If it's a one-time incident and a bit uncharacteristic of him, you can certainly let it go and not mention a thing. That's called serving one another. However, if you feel a conversation is needed, you can certainly discuss what happened. Here's the key: If you approach the conversation with a forgiving heart, you'll more likely be able to resolve the conflict swiftly. However, if you approach the conversation filled with anger, you'll put your husband on the defense and make little progress in resolving the conflict. In fact, it will probably become bigger than it really needed to be.

Marriage isn't the only place conflict happens. Similar scenarios are played out every day with our children, our neighbors, and our friends. We have to learn to recognize the dozens of Y's in the road we face every day living life with other people. Once we do we can begin to teach our children, both by direct instruction and by example, the beauty of living by grace. Each family member needs to understand the concept of forgiveness and grace to make home where we not only feel safe from criticism, but also celebrated for who we are—mistakes and all.

I'm still on the grace journey. I've come a long way from the anger and criticism in the early years of marriage and mothering, but I still blow it sometimes. You will too. When we do, we take a step back, clean up the relational mess ("I'm sorry. Will you please forgive me?"), and allow the incident to be a reminder to watch for the Y's in the road of life.

Intentionally Listen

"Mom, can we talk?" That's a question most of us long to hear from our kids. It's hard for a kid to ask that even in the best relational environment, but it's nearly impossible for them to ask that when they anticipate the response will be a lecture, a dozen ways to solve the problem, or out-and-out anger. As a parent, there are two questions we need to ask ourselves: "Am I a good listener?" and "Am I a safe person to talk to?"

Learning to listen is one of the most important skills in which a parent can grow. How we listen will determine whether a person feels heard, valued, and respected. Many years ago, four-year-old Austin was telling me a story while I prepared dinner. He sat at the island in the kitchen while I moved from the refrigerator to the sink to the pantry and back again. As Austin talked, I gave some verbal responses to let him know I was listening. But that wasn't enough. Finally he interrupted his story and said with frustration, "Mom, will you listen to me?" I told him I was listening and even repeated part of the story back to him. He responded with, "No, don't just listen with your ears. Listen to me with your eyes." Wow. There's nothing like a life lesson from your four-year-old.

We can remember the three keys to listening well with three words: Stop, Look, and Listen.

- STOP everything you are doing and turn your body toward the person talking.

- LOOK in their eyes to give value and affirmation as they speak.

- LISTEN intently and refrain from using your mouth except to encourage.

If they are facing a problem that needs to be solved, you might ask, "Are you looking for solutions or do you just need me to listen?" This helps clarify what your spouse or child is looking for from you as they vent. It also makes you a better listener and makes them feel you are a safe person to talk to.

If your child needs to cry, then hold them and let them cry. Don't try to solve their problems. Pray with them. Comfort them. Let them know that you wish you could take away the hurt, but since you can't, you'll walk the journey alongside them.

If your child isn't willing to talk but seems to be slipping into depression or withdrawing, find someone they can talk with. Don't be offended by their difficulty in sharing with you. Show them you care by getting some help. One mom shared with me how her daughter was beginning to show signs of depression and was withdrawing from family relationships. She contacted a counselor and set up an appointment. At first the daughter didn't want to go, but Mom gently persisted. In time the counselor's office became a safe place and provided the daughter a place to talk during a difficult season of her teen years.

When home is a safe house, it is a place where we feel safe to communicate what we are struggling with or feeling without judgment, criticism, or ten easy answers to our problem. If I'm a safe person to talk to, my child can trust that I will listen to them, won't explode or overreact, and will bite my tongue occasionally and refrain from trying to solve all their problems. This type of environment builds safety and trust in a family and makes home a safe place to be.

Increase Margin

When Dr. Richard Swenson wrote the book *Margin,* he likened certain areas of our lives to the margins—or white space—in a book. His premise is that society's fast pace has decreased the white space in our life to a level that is dangerous for both our physical and relational health. We'll explore this more in chapter 2, but I mention it here because adequate margins are needed for home to be a safe house. Home is a safe place to be when there is a balance between doing and being, work and rest, going and staying home.

Kids need balance in their schedules, leaving a large amount of white space for running, playing, and using their imagination. They also need adequate sleep and occasional naps. Margin is not only essential for kids, it's important for parents too. Pace of life has a lot to do with a mom's ability to offer grace and forgiveness. Both forgiveness and grace require emotional energy on our part. If we are emotionally spent, we're going to be far less patient, less forgiving, and less grace-filled than we need to be. If you are in the baby/toddler stage of life, napping when the baby naps may be a necessity to have the emotional energy you need for the remainder of the day. If your children are older, you may find it necessary to simplify your schedule or their schedule to allow for more positive family interaction.

Turn Sibling Rivalry into Sibling Revelry

In his book *Keep the Siblings, Lose the Rivalry,* Todd Cartmell tells us there are three reasons for sibling rivalry:

Reason #3: You have more than one child.

Reason #2: Your children live in the same house.

Reason #1: Your children's living-together skills are still developing.[1]

There's not too much a parent can do about reasons 2 and 3, but some intentional strategy in approaching reason 1 is what will turn sibling rivalry into sibling revelry and ultimately make home a safe place to be.

Strategy 1: Play Together

Every child longs to belong. When families intentionally spend time together, they increase the family bond, ultimately helping each family member feel a part of something bigger than themselves. As parents, we need to create a "we are a team" mind-set that casts a vision for each family member to be a part of a team designed to last a lifetime.

Strategy 2: Connect Individually

Children won't vie for your attention if they know they have it already. I once heard author and speaker Elise Arndt, a mother of five, say that one goal a mom should have is to occasionally make each child feel like an only child. Mark and I have found that to be a reachable goal, and we have worked to accomplish it by taking the kids out on dates with one or both of us, taking them school shopping by themselves, spending time lying on their bed at night talking, and making sure we are in attendance at any event they are involved in.

Strategy 3: Set Clear Standards and Expectations

Most of the time, kids will rise to the standard you set. When we deal with misbehavior, it is often because the child is looking for the boundary line. Let your family know that sibling respect is the standard in your family. Discuss what is expected of them in attending one another's extracurricular activities. You might want to occasionally call family meetings to set standards or call everyone back to a standard that seems to be slipping. You might also brainstorm as to how you can celebrate and support one another—letting the entire family help set the standard and come up with ways to carry it out.

Strategy 4: Model Healthy Conflict Resolution Skills

If Joey and Suzie see Mom and Dad yell and scream at one another in conflict, you can almost bet that, when conflict happens between the two siblings, they'll be yelling and screaming before you know it. If you and your spouse don't resolve conflict in a healthy way, seek out help in developing conflict management skills that will take your marriage the distance and foster healthy family relationships.

Mark and I had to do this ourselves as we came from opposite ends of the spectrum when it came to resolving conflict. One of us raged and one of us tried to sweep things under the carpet. Neither method was healthy, so we sought out a marriage counselor who helped us find middle ground—a strategy that fostered communication, helped us feel heard, allowed for compromise and agreement, and brought closure and healing to places we had wounded one another in the process. We learned the value of a whole apology ("I'm sorry. Will you please forgive me?" "Yes, I forgive you.") that needed to happen when we hurt one another.

Strategy 5: Teach Healthy Conflict Resolution Skills

Once Mom and Dad learn healthy conflict resolution skills, it's time to talk about it with the kids. Even if bad conflict resolution habits have invaded your home, it's never too late to apologize for being poor role models, explain what you've learned, and set new standards in place that will preserve relationships over the long haul. You might even do some role-playing with your kids to illustrate what needs to happen to make things right with another family member when someone has been intentionally or unintentionally hurt.

Make It Safe to Fail

"Failure is simply an indicator that a child needs more time to develop. If your child is going to fail—and roughly 100 percent do—you want him or her to learn to fail gracefully in the safety of your home," says Dr. Kevin Leman.[2]

Kids need to know that taking risks and failing is a natural part of life. Failing doesn't define a person; it simply clarifies their skill level and indicates places they need to grow. We want our kids to know that home is the safest place to fall because someone will always be there to help them back up.

An important key in making home a safe place to fail is for us, as parents, to realize that a child's failure does not define us as well. When Austin was four years old, he embarrassed me in public. I found myself shaming him for his childish behavior, hoping that I could bring about compliance so that I could look better. But God spoke to me in that moment and reminded me that my self-worth is not based upon my child's behavior. My value and self-worth are based upon my relationship with God. Once that truth moved from my head to my heart, I knew that a new level of safety had been created in our home.

How about you? Have you ever found yourself more concerned with how you appear to others than how you are treating a family member who has disappointed you or failed in some way? The only way you can keep from making the same mistake I did is to remember that your value and your self-worth are not dependent upon how you look or how your family looks or behaves. That's building your life on sinking sand.

What we have to do is build our lives on a Solid Rock—Someone who never changes and is the same yesterday, today, and tomorrow. It is only then that we'll be able to allow family members to fail in an emotionally safe environment.

A Foundation of Safety

This year on my birthday I received a priceless gift from my 15-year-old daughter, who was coming out of a very difficult and tumultuous year of her teenage life. She took a picture of herself and framed it with the following words:

> Mom, I am so grateful for all the years you have invested into my life. Thank you…for so many hours spent with me when I was sick…for crying with me when I just needed to cry…for loving me even when it was incredibly hard… for being patient with me when you just wanted to yell at me…for spending time with me when I needed it the

most…for going to all my games and supporting me in my decisions…for listening to me when I felt like no one could hear me…for not giving up when times were hard.

You have shown me how to live as an amazing woman of God. Your life has become a stencil of Christ's love. May these words truly convey how much I love you.

Learning to be safe has been a 21-year journey for me as a mother. I still mess up sometimes, but I'm making progress—at least enough progress that Erica was able to feel loved, cared for, and essentially safe even during a difficult period of her life.

The foundational elements are relationship driven with the intention of establishing, preserving, deepening, and protecting family relationships. Healthy relationships set us on our relationship track for the rest of their lives. The relationships we have with our parents and our siblings serve as the foundation for all future relationships in life. It's far more important that children grow up in an emotionally safe home than it is that they have opportunities for lessons, sports, or other activities that are considered an essential part of childhood. We start by making home a safe house and then we build from there.

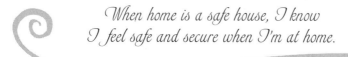

When home is a safe house, I know
I feel safe and secure when I'm at home.

~ 2 ~

Home as a Rest Area

*If I were asked to name the chief benefit of the house, I should
say: the house shelters day-dreaming, the house protects
the dreamer, the house allows one to dream in peace.*

GASTON BACHELARD

M ark and I approach road trips very differently. He drinks lots
of coffee and figures a rest stop every hour is just part of a
trip. I, on the other hand, try to make as few stops as possible. My
goal is to arrive at our destination in the quickest, most efficient
way possible.

We approach life the way we do road trips. I always have a to-
do list in my head. Mark does too, but he almost always has "take
a nap" on every to-do list. They say that married couples should
allow their differences to complete and complement one another.
Often we can learn from our differences. In our case, I've been able
to learn from Mark when to slow down and make home the rest
area it needs to be.

Watch Your Speed

A highway speed of 65 mph is considered standard in the United
States. Some states even allow speeds of 70 or 75 mph. That's traveling along at a pretty good clip.

We can't keep up that speed forever. Eventually we have to stop,
get a bite to eat, fill the gas tank, and clean the windshield. We've

got to exit the highway and make a rest stop to give us the fuel (both for our body and for our car) to take us the distance.

Our lives work the same way. The pace of life we travel at breaks all speed barriers from generations past. We work long hours, pack in too many activities, say yes too often, and often push ourselves so hard that we end up broken-down on the side of the road.

Mary Steinke, in her newspaper article entitled "The Hurried Family," states that "being in a hurry comes naturally to families today":

- Our culture values speed. ATMs. Fast food. E-mail.
- The workplace rewards hurriedness. Overtime. Working weekends. Beepers.
- The media encourages haste. Instant news. Instant hit shows. Instant Internet info.[1]

Indeed, we live in a fast-paced culture. Could it be, however, that while the world is traveling at breakneck speeds, we could choose to operate at a slower pace of life? We tell our kids not to cave in to peer pressure, but we are tempted to do so ourselves as we try to keep up with the neighbors, give our kids the best, or take advantage of every opportunity offered. We do have choices about how we use our time. Sometimes we're just not aware of the choices we have.

Slow Down and Let Kids Be Kids

Parents often ask me, as a former piano teacher, when they should begin their child in piano lessons. When I recommend no earlier than second grade, they are amazed.

Part of my answer comes from my experience teaching young children and finding that second grade is the earliest most children have the ability to sit still to practice and have the reading abilities that allow them to read music. The other reason I suggest second grade comes from what I've learned as a parent and the tendency we have to want to get our child involved in organized activities much earlier than they need to be.

In *Primary Psychiatry* magazine, Alvin Rosenfeld and Nicole Wise, the authors of an article titled "Let Kids Be Kids: Avoiding the Hyper-Parenting Trap," coined the phrase "hyper-parenting" to describe a trend they are seeing in parenting more and more often. It seems today's parents are making it their sacred responsibility to provide their child with every enrichment opportunity possible: sports, music, academics, etc.

At the same time, the medical and psychiatric industry are seeing an increase in children's stress factors because activities have so filled their calendars that they are overwhelmed and even sleep deprived. Why do we do this as parents? Because we want to give our children the best. However, sometimes we're missing what really is best.

Dr. Kevin Leman tells the story of a four-year-old boy playing outfield in a T-ball game. When the ball came his way, the crowd yelled for him to get the ball. However, this little guy was on the ground on his hands and knees searching desperately for something in the grass. He was completely oblivious to the ballgame he was supposed to be playing. When his father yelled for him to get the ball, little Joey looked up and said, "I can't get the ball. I'm looking for a four-leaf clover!"

Kids need to have enough margin in their life to look for four-leaf clovers. Building sand castles, flying kites, or playing a game of tag in the backyard—these are the activities kids need to do in the preschool and early elementary years. Play is a child's work, and their days need to be full of it. There is plenty of time for organized sports and lessons later in grade school, junior high, and high school. I consider it a great accomplishment when my young sons smell like "sweaty boy" at the end of a day. I know they've played hard and accomplished much with a mixture of imagination, energy, and passion for their "work."

Rosenfeld and Wise indicate that for some of us parenting has become America's most competitive adult sport. "Parents have come to see a child's success quantified by 'achievements' like speaking early or qualifying for the gifted and talented program at school as the measure of parental success...They have come to believe that it is activities and accomplishments, not warm relationships, that make a child 'successful' in life."[2]

How can we steer clear of the hyper-parenting trap? We need to focus on relationships and more time with our families, not more activities that distract us from what is really important in life. Though activities do help children identify their gifts, talents, and abilities, the key is finding a balance in the load of activities being carried as well as carefully considering the age at which they are introduced. Here are some principles for keeping a balance:

- *Assess age-appropriateness.* Just because a program offers classes for toddlers doesn't mean toddlers need to take classes. We need to be careful about making children grow up too fast.

- *Limit activities.* Some families make firm rules (that is, one sport per child per season) while others make decisions on a case-by-case basis. "Weigh the benefit against the cost (time, energy, logistical effort, stress, expense) to you, your child, and the family,"[3] suggest Rosenfeld and Wise.

- *Prioritize family.* Relationships matter…a lot. Our families need to know how to play together, not just ride in the car together from one activity to the next. Consider making one night a week family night. Set aside time to play sports or board games, go fishing, or just relax and talk with one another.

- *Refrain from activity overload.* Boredom needs to be a goal of parents. Unscheduled time encourages children to create and imagine. It helps them to learn how to fill their time rather than expect others to entertain them.

As parents, one of our jobs is to help our children learn to manage their time, resources, and abilities. In these things, more is caught than taught. They will learn by watching us manage our lives as well as experiencing the schedule we create for them. Let's let kids be kids in the early years of their lives. It will set a foundation of balance that will serve them well into adulthood. By the way, American composer and conductor Leonard Bernstein didn't sit down at a piano before his tenth birthday. So you see, second grade isn't too late after all.

By letting kids be kids, we allow for margin in our time and pace of life. But there are other kinds of margin to consider, including emotional and physical margin.

Emotional Margin

Emotional margin allows for laughter and tears. It's refueled by both time alone and friendships. Ultimately, it allows us to confront life's challenges with a sense of hope and power. A family with emotional margin laughs together a lot. They enjoy telling stories and laughing at punch lines. There is a sense of joy in their home. At the same time, a safe home with balanced emotional margin allows family members to grieve over the disappointments of life. Shedding tears is seen as a God-given way of expressing emotion for Mom and Dad, sons and daughters.

Emotional margin is refueled by time with God, time with friends, and time alone. When we spend time in prayer and reading God's Word, we are empowered with perspective, truth, and hope. Prayer is simply talking with God: praising Him for who He is, finding forgiveness in confession, expressing thanks for answered prayer and His provision, and lifting up our needs and asking for His guidance in the journey of life. The Bible is full of life-giving truth as well as direction for our life. When we read the Bible, we find God's perspective, which often adjusts our off-centered perspective. We also find truth that gives us direction and a never-changing standard for attitudes and actions. Finally we find hope, especially when life feels hopeless or empty. When we have hope, we're able to meet whatever challenges life brings our way.

When I spend a couple hours talking to my friend Doris, it's like pulling up to a filling station and filling my emotional gas tank. Friends fill us up—they laugh with us, cry with us, and just make life more enjoyable and fun. When Jesus lived on this earth, He lived with His disciples—they were His friends. He modeled for us our need for relationships—friends who journey through life with us.

We need time with God and time with friends, but we also need time alone. When it feels as though everyone wants a piece of you and the world is pulling at you from all directions, time alone is restorative. With all of my children in school, I find this time during the day when I'm home alone. However, I have to be more strategic to find it in the summer months when everyone is home. I particularly remember when our first three were very young and I was craving some time alone. I finally asked my husband if he would give me 30 minutes of alone time after he got home from work. I had dinner cooking, and he'd arrive home and take over with the kids for 30 minutes. I would go to our bedroom and close the door and read the newspaper. After 30 minutes, I felt like a new person. I had pulled off the highway to the rest area of my bedroom and found the emotional refreshment I needed.

Physical Margin

Physical margin happens when we have a healthy balance of exercise, nutrition, and rest. Only a body that is well rested, properly exercised, and correctly fed will be able to maintain its energy reserves in the face of serious stress.[4] Our body is an amazing gift. If we feed it, water it, rest it, and move it, we will find energy we never knew we had![5] Moms find this kind of margin one of the hardest to balance. When you are up with a baby in the night, or consider the crusts of your toddler's peanut butter sandwich your lunch for the day, physical margin is compromised.

As a mom, I've found that walking is the most affordable exercise—walk the mall, walk a trail, walk around a park—any walking for 20 to 30 minutes a day is a good start to the exercise your body needs. If you belong to a local gym, utilize the child care they offer and set a regular routine for a cardiovascular and muscle-toning workout. A new mom stopped me at one of our Hearts at Home conferences and said, "Jill, you need to talk to moms more about getting regular exercise. After I had my baby, I found myself irritable and even depressed. Out of desperation I found an affordable gym that offered child care services, and I began going almost daily. That little bit of time I take for myself has made all the difference in the world for my attitude and perspective." Exercise is not only for our body, but for our mind as well.

When it comes to nutrition, we need to consider not only the food we eat but the water we drink too. Keep a glass of ice and water going all day to remind you to keep your body hydrated. If you like water with lemon, grab a lemon each time you're at the grocery store and keep it cut up in an airtight container in the refrigerator. This will allow you to grab a lemon slice each time you fix yourself a glass of water. Do the same with healthy snacks such as carrot and celery sticks, cheese slices, or fruit, such as cantaloupe or honeydew melon. It takes a little bit of work right after you come home from the grocery store, but it makes it so much easier to grab healthy food when it is ready to eat. Meals should consist of plenty of fruits and vegetables. Try to use fresh whenever possible to maximize the nutrients in the food. Frozen and canned foods are fine occasionally, but they give us more sodium and often a large dose of preservatives that our body doesn't need.

When it comes to rest, naps are perfectly acceptable for a tired mom. When your baby sleeps, you may need to sleep too. Our family sets aside Sunday afternoon as a time of rest. Mark and I and our teens routinely take at least a two-hour nap, while our grade-schoolers have time alone in their bedroom to read and play quietly. It's a much-needed part of giving our body the care it needs. Getting good rest at night is important too. Bedtime is such a struggle for me. I'm a night owl and often stay up too late for the time my body needs to get up in the morning, but I'm learning how important it is to make sure I'm conscious of the physical margin I need in my life and how important rest is to keep it all in balance.

The Family Meal

As a mother, there are many days that I long to leave the kitchen for more than 30 minutes. When everyone is home throughout the day, it feels as though we move from breakfast to a midmorning snack, then lunch and an afternoon snack, and then dinner and a bedtime snack. Could we just consider the kitchen closed for a few hours? When I find myself frustrated with the amount of time I spend there, I realize I need to adjust my perspective.

While mealtimes have nutritional purposes, they also serve a larger purpose of building community within a family. When the family sits down together to share a meal, it is as if they pull off the highway of life, find a parking spot, and enjoy relational refreshment.

Family identity is increased when families eat meals together. The conversations around the table build bonds that last a lifetime. Families that eat together know what's happening in each other's lives. They are connected, concerned, and conscious of the other members of the family. My friend Sylvia remembers mealtimes as a child. "Whenever I think of home, I think of us around the dinner table. There's nothing that can replace the intimacy that happens around the dinner table."

According to a recent article I read, the National Center on Addiction and Substance Abuse at Columbia University has research to support that teens who ate dinner five to seven times a week with their families were 45 percent less likely to try alcohol, 24 percent less apt to smoke marijuana, and 67 percent more likely to get A's compared with kids who never or rarely dined with their families. This illustrates that the benefits of the family meal are far-reaching and all-encompassing in a child's life.

But how can you get a meal on the table when you feel overwhelmed with the prospect of making that happen? Here are some practical tips to help you succeed in making a meal you can share together:

- *Create a monthly meal plan with your family's favorite meals.* This strategy of "advance decision making" helps eliminate the "what should I make for dinner" question each night. A meal plan also streamlines your shopping list when you head to the grocery store.

- *Use your Crock-Pot whenever possible.* This helps you prepare your meals during less hectic times of the day. It also fills the house with wonderful smells that communicate that all is well, Mom is in charge, and dinner is being prepared.

- *Have a stash of freezer meals from which to choose.* You might try "one-a-month cooking" where you cook for a day to eat for a month! There are hundreds of resources available to show you how to successfully cook once a month. Type "once-a-month cooking" into your Internet search engine, and you'll find all the resources you need.

- *Make double or prepare partially.* When I make meatloaf for our family, I make one meatloaf for our evening meal and two for the freezer. I do the same with our family's favorite casseroles. You can also do partial preparation to simplify meal prep later. For instance, each month I buy hamburger in bulk. When I get home I divide it and use half for meatloaf and meatballs that I will prepare and freeze (uncooked). The other half of the hamburger I brown with a little bit of onion, salt, and pepper. Of the browned hamburger, I freeze half in freezer bags for dishes such as chili, sloppy joes, or beef stroganoff. I then season the remaining browned meat with taco seasoning and place it in freezer bags for our favorite Mexican meals. When I decide to have tacos for dinner, I simply pull the bag of seasoned meat out of the freezer and microwave it until it thaws enough to be placed in a bowl. I then thoroughly heat it in the bowl until it is at serving temperature. This minimizes cleanup and cuts close to 30 minutes off my prep time.

- *Make meal prep and setting the table a family event.* The family meal is more likely to happen if the responsibility is shared by all who will eat. Whether you have a schedule for who helps with dinner or sets the table, or you determine that 15 minutes before a meal everyone works together to make it happen, make sure you share the ownership of the family meal.

- *Make cleanup a family event.* If I clean up alone after a meal, it usually takes about 30 minutes. If we all work together, the task is finished within an average of 10 minutes. Require everyone to clear their own plates and help clear the table, wipe the counters, sweep the floor, and fill the dishwasher or wash dishes. This provides opportunity for the family to work together each evening.

Once you sit down for the meal, take time for intentional communication. Create a tradition of having each person share while you eat. If your family is not accustomed to doing this, it might feel awkward at first, but before long it will become part of the fabric of your family life. Here are some ideas to get you started:

- Tell us about the worst part of your day and the best part of your day.
- What is one thing you are looking forward to in the next week?
- Tell us about your day in chronological order.
- What is one thing we can pray about for you?

Make sure Mom and Dad share right along with the kids. You want to know your kids, but your kids need to know you too. By slowing down the meal process and sharing about yourselves, you are intentionally building community and deepening family relationships.

Family Night

It's late afternoon on Sunday. Anne is in her bedroom reading, Evan is on the computer, Erica is doing a craft project, and Austin and Kolya are outside shooting baskets. Mark and I are discussing our plans for family night. Our goal is to pull everyone from their corners and facilitate some time in an activity that builds relationship. It's an effort that is not always met with a "hip-hip-hurray" response, but by the end of the evening the feedback rings in with a very positive tone.

When Mark and I began evaluating our parenting role several years ago, we determined that we wanted to "parent on purpose." We wanted to have a plan for raising our children, so we made sure certain ingredients were present in our family's habits. Our desire was to look forward and plan our approach now, rather than look back in 18 years and regret a lack of direction and purpose. In order to take this proactive approach, we have worked hard to mesh our two lives and two different upbringings into a parenting philosophy we can both agree upon. It's not been an easy road, but one I'm glad we took. The most effective tool for us was our own desire to learn. We read books, asked questions, attended conferences, talked about our own upbringing, and took several parenting classes. And we continue to do so as we enter into even more uncharted waters of raising children. Along the way, we were introduced to the concept of family night. It was a concept that was new to both of us, but one we were drawn to.

In recent years, we've established Sunday night as our traditional family night. It seems to consistently be an evening we can protect and use to the fullest. In the beginning, our family night schedule was flexible. We began our evenings by preparing everyone days in advance, if possible. Occasionally we would find everyone home and decide to do a more spontaneous evening. In that case we would call out "Family fun in 30 minutes!" to give everyone a chance to wrap up their activities and look forward to something we would do together. Family nights never look exactly the same, but the results are consistent. We are closer, communicating better, and have the sense of being teammates.

If you've never done a family night, here are some tried-and-true tips to successfully pull the family together:

- If possible, set aside one night of the week that becomes sacred to your family. No one accepts an invitation that evening, no meetings, no social engagements—it's reserved for family night.

- If setting aside one night a week is not feasible with your family's schedule, sit down with the calendar and plan for some evenings together. Communicate to everyone these dates and keep them free from activities.

- Include the kids in planning the activities. When they feel they have been valued in the planning process, their desire to participate increases.

- Don't be discouraged if the process of gathering everyone is met with frustration, especially early on. We all have a self-centered nature and have to be coached into understanding the importance of team.

- Be creative with your evenings: game night (Scrabble, Monopoly, Pictionary), watching home movies, going through old photo albums, watching a movie together, baking cookies. Bowling, miniature golf, ice-skating, and roller-skating make for enjoyable family time too.

- Don't discount the ability to do family night even if your children have a wide age range. One summer we took the kids golfing (this was a "family morning") at the Par 3 golf course. Our older children were able to golf while our two-year-old enjoyed the ride in the wagon we brought with us.

As parents, we have only one shot at raising our kids. It's not a job we can do over again. That's why activities that build into the family relationship are so very important. Family nights are one way we slow down the pace of life and find refreshment in the relationships of family.

Family Vacation

Everybody needs "time away from the everyday" according to Allie Pleiter in her Hearts at Home book *Becoming a Chief Home Officer.*[6] Families need time to step away from the everyday responsibilities of life to play, relax, and have fun together.

When I was growing up, family vacations consisted of going to see another part of the country and, rather than Holiday Inn, we looked for KOA so we could plop down our tent and sleep for the night. I enjoyed those vacations—they were all I knew a vacation could be.

Quite a few years ago my parents purchased a condo in Fort Walton Beach, Florida, and they have been very gracious to share it with us. Because it is an economical vacation for our family of seven, most summers we spend a week on the beach in Florida. When I suggested making a road trip to Yellowstone Park last summer rather than going to the beach, the kids loudly protested. "Mom, that wouldn't be a family vacation. That would be a family field trip. We need a vacation!"

Sometimes our children teach us so much. They were completely right. We needed a break, a time to rest, not a seven-day sightseeing schedule across the country. Don't get me wrong. If those are the kinds of vacations your family enjoys and needs—then go for it! For us, however, it would have defeated the purpose of a vacation that we needed as a family. We needed to "get away from the everyday" and really rest, relax, and rejuvenate.

If your family doesn't take a family vacation each summer, consider the value of doing so. It doesn't have to cost a lot; it just needs to get you away from daily routines. Maybe it's camping at a state park over a long weekend or finding an inexpensive hotel with a pool on Priceline.com. Whatever it is, there are memories to be made, fun to be had, and rest to be found when you slow down enough to step away from the everyday.

The Lost Art of Neighboring and Porching

My friend Rita described a recent afternoon in her neighborhood. After a powerful storm had passed through the area, the neighborhood was left without electricity. With nothing to do inside, everyone began to meander out into the street, visiting with one another and watching their kids play in the puddles. She said it was such a nice time chatting with neighbors she rarely saw on a daily basis.

After about 20 minutes, porch lights came on as evidence that the electricity had been restored. As soon as people realized that their power was back on, they immediately excused themselves to head back inside. Rita found herself marveling at how quickly people had left the community gathering in the street to the isolation of their home.

Gone are the days where neighboring is an American pastime.

Our lives move so quickly from one activity to another that the most interaction we have with our neighbors is a quick wave on the way in or on the way out of the driveway.

Dr. John Buchino, author of *Porching: A Humorous Look at America's Favorite Pastime,* says that porching has medical benefits, including lowering blood pressure and prolonging life. Architect Russel Francois believes air-conditioning and attached garages brought a slow death to porching. He said today's homeowners rarely look at porches for lingering but more for curb appeal. The porch is a tool, but if we don't have the energy to socialize, we won't use it. Sitting there encourages interaction, and by the time we finally get home at night, most of us would rather retreat indoors and be entertained rather than be entertaining.[7]

Several years after we bought our farmhouse, we decided to finally tackle the front porch. When we bought the house, the porch was caved in and the front door had been caulked shut. Because we had so much to renovate and restore, the front porch was one of the last big jobs we had to tackle. The weekend we tore off the old porch I noted how cold and unwelcoming the house looked without it. (Even though the old porch had been unusable, it had still protected the front of the house and given it a completed look.) Over a long weekend, we built a full-size wraparound porch on the front of our home. That porch has become another room in our house during the summer months. We visit with friends, take afternoon naps, and even eat meals there. In the evening after the kids are in bed, Mark and I often enjoy a minidate, snuggling on the porch swing and talking about life.

Front porch (or back porch) sitting, also called porching, is a pastime worth reviving. It slows down life enough to ponder, visit, and even watch a thunderstorm roll in. If you have a front porch and it's an inviting place to be, porching might open the door to neighboring. A neighbor walking by just might bring about some impromptu conversations and an invitation to come sit and chat awhile. Back porches are more isolated and usually require more of an invitation to visit, but those conversations are just as valuable.

Because we live out in the country, our neighbors don't just walk by on the sidewalk. We have to extend an invite or be ready for unexpected company—either are fine with us. We just enjoy the slower pace that the porch invites us to enjoy.

Exit the Highway

Mark and I may have different traveling perspectives, but one thing we agree upon is the need to exit the highway when nature calls. Once the car is parked everyone stretches their legs, finds the bathroom, and takes a much-needed break from the cramped and crowded conditions in the car.

The principles are the same as we travel through life. We have to regularly exit the highway to take a much-needed break from the duties and demands in everyday life. We have to maintain balance in our lives to go the distance physically and emotionally…and home is just the place to do that.

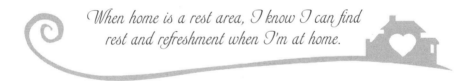

When home is a rest area, I know I can find rest and refreshment when I'm at home.

3

Home as a Trauma Unit

*Home is the place that'll catch you when
you fall. And we all fall.*

BILLIE LETTS

Erica barely made it through the senior event we attended for Evan. Her older brother and sister had both attended University High School—a school in our community associated with Illinois State University. U-High is a public school, but one with limited admission numbers. Both Anne and Evan had applied to attend during their eighth grade year and were invited to be a part of the school. Our family had been a part of the school for six years, and Erica knew U-High was where she would go too. She also applied in her eighth grade year and waited for her acceptance letter.

The day the letter arrived from U-High she was so excited to open it. However, the moment she read the first few lines, tears began to run down her cheeks. She had not been invited to be a part of their next freshman class. She was devastated. Her dreams of following in her brother and sister's footsteps were crushed.

The letter arrived one month before her brother's high school graduation. Every event we attended for Evan reopened Erica's wounds of disappointment and rejection. She was hurting and in great emotional pain. She needed home to be a trauma unit.

The Healing Environment

When an accident happens and physical healing needs to take place, several elements create an environment conducive to healing. The hospital is a protective setting where medication, equipment, and knowledgeable staff are readily available. It is a place where one is separated from the routine and responsibilities of daily life so the body can rest, recuperate, and begin to heal. When home is a trauma unit, it becomes a safe place for emotions to be expressed, grief to be experienced, and the healing process to begin.

Doctors and nurses administer medicine and care when illness or injury invades our body. When home is a trauma unit, Mom, Dad, and siblings become the trauma team to administer love, lend a listening ear, share the disappointment and grief, and encourage healing and hope in due time.

A family that shares each other's pain is a tight, close-knit family. When family members are allowed to express their emotions and not encouraged to just "buck up and move on," then home becomes a safe place to be sad, disappointed, or even angry. A healthy trauma team encourages the wounded member to process, grieve, and eventually find closure to the hurt that has happened.

Let's examine the responsibilities of the trauma team when crisis hits a family member.

Administer Love

When hurt poisons our lives, the only antidote for that poison is love. Love says, "I care." It is gentle and kind. Love doesn't demand its own way, but comes alongside and walks through the hurt with the other person. God describes love in what has become known as the "Love Chapter" of the Bible, 1 Corinthians 13:

> Love is patient, love is kind. It does not envy, it does not boast, it is not proud. It is not rude, it is not self-seeking, it is not easily angered, it keeps no record of wrongs. Love does not delight in evil but rejoices with the truth. It always protects, always trusts, always hopes, and always perseveres. Love never fails (1 Corinthians 13:4-8).

Contrary to popular belief, love isn't a feeling. Love is a choice. It is a verb—an action word. When home is a trauma unit, sometimes that is the most important and yet most challenging time to love. When someone is hurting they don't always act right—they can become somewhat unlovable. However, that's when God wants to hone our own character and show us that with His help we can love even in the most difficult situations.

Lend a Listening Ear

When we hurt, we need to sort through the emotions. Many times we experience a whole array of feelings about the situation, but those feelings are all jumbled together in our mind. When someone provides a listening ear and asks questions to draw us out, we progress toward healing.

Learning to listen without trying to fix the hurt is one of the hardest things to do. One of the first places to start is by learning to ask questions. Jesus was a master at this. He didn't always give the answer (though He knew it!); rather, He helped draw people to the conclusion themselves.

I've found professional counseling to be helpful during difficult seasons of my life. When you spend much time in a counselor's office, you start noticing how many questions they ask you: "What did you think about that?" "What was that experience like?" "How did that make you feel?" Their job is to make you think about your feelings and connect you to your emotions. They draw you out and help you walk along a path to healing.

If a member of your family is in trauma, they need you to be like a counselor: listen intently and ask questions to help them sort through their feelings. Refrain from giving them pat answers or solutions to the problem. It's okay to let them *feel* and for you to have empathy and *feel* along with them. This is particularly hard for those of us with a type A personality who want to "do" more than "be." However, it is a skill we can hone and a place we can become more Christlike.

Being a member of a trauma team means you have to know

when a specialist needs to be called in. When the hurt is extremely deep or the "down feeling" has moved into depression, a trained counselor or medical doctor may need to be part of the trauma team. Getting professional help is a sign of strength and a viable option when dealing with intense emotional pain.

Allow for Disappointment and Grief

In *The Emotionally Healthy Church*, Peter Scazzaro states, "Few Christians in North America and Europe understand sorrow and grieving, especially as it relates to God, ourselves, and its vital importance to living in healthy community. But the degree to which I learn to grieve my own losses is in direct proportion to the depth and quality of my relationship with God and the compassion I can offer to others."[1]

When Tricia was a child, she grew up in a great family, and she was always free to express her emotions anytime she needed to. However, as an adult Tricia found herself sitting in a counselor's office trying to figure out why she was so closed off to intimate friendships. As she dug into her past, she realized that while her family taught her many healthy perspectives about emotion, they rarely discussed how they actually *felt* about anything. She could remember several family crises where the family came together and got through the crisis but never discussed how they felt during the situation. They simply had the perspective that "This is life. We do what we can to survive it and we move on." There was rarely a pausing in life for celebrating or grieving. And now, as an adult, she operated very much in the same way.

If home is to be a trauma unit, we have to allow time and space to grieve our losses. Feeling the pain of disappointment or hurt and grieving our pain and losses keep us from building emotional walls. Grief actually expands our heart, increases our mercy, and grows our compassion for others.

Jesus said, "Blessed are those who mourn, for they will be comforted" (Matthew 5:4). Grief is a normal part of life. When trauma hits, the trauma team listens, loves, and comforts while allowing the family member to hurt, grieve, and lament their loss.

Encourage Healing and Hope

After loving, listening, and grieving, we can then begin to look at the future and consider hope again—but not until we've been given time for our mind and body to heal from the hurt we've experienced. Many times this is where a trauma team fails to successfully move a person from hurt to healing. Often a team member wants to jump from hurt to hope, bypassing the healing steps of loving, listening, and grieving. When we short-circuit the healing process, several things can happen:

We search for a substitute. Where do family members go for trauma care when the home doesn't provide it? A teenager might turn to their peers looking for someone to love and listen. A family member might turn to alcohol or drugs to deaden the emotional pain they feel. A spouse might look for another person of the opposite sex to love and listen, which is how affairs often begin.

We turn off our emotions. When a child or young adult experiences several life traumas without their emotions being acknowledged, they begin to believe that feelings don't really matter. In time they accommodate to their surroundings by turning off their need to feel.

We accumulate losses. When a person is never allowed to feel, grieve, or express their emotions, they begin to accumulate losses over a lifetime. An accumulation of losses without the ability to process those losses eventually becomes like an emotional wall—a coping mechanism that a person latches onto to protect them from future hurt. As an adult they may end up in a counselor's office trying to figure out why they seem distant from their spouse or why they find it difficult to be vulnerable with friends.

We need to allow our children, our spouse, and ourselves to experience all the steps of the healing process. After that has happened, a wounded person can begin to think about hope again. They can begin to see how God will use hurt to help them grow or help others in their life journey. And if we have loved, listened, and grieved along with them, we've then earned the right to help them hope again.

The Power of Prayer

Throughout a healing process, prayer is the most essential element. We can't love the way God wants us to love without His help. We can't listen and have the self-control to refrain from trying to fix the person or the problem without His wisdom. We can't find the patience to wade through the grief and disappointment on our own without His strength. And we can't hope without knowing God's promises that He will redeem and restore.

If the hurting family member will allow you to pray with them along every part of the journey, then make prayer a part of what you do together. That may be a new experience for you, but it is freeing to learn to take our mountains to the Mountain Mover. Prayer doesn't need to be a formal event. God just wants us to talk with Him the way we would talk with a friend. Think about this: When God sent His Son, Jesus, to live on this earth, He was fully God, yet fully man. That means that God, through His Son, experienced both emotional and physical pain. He was let down by His friends. He was betrayed. He knows the hurt of disappointment and rejection. He experienced horrendous physical pain upon the cross. He understands all the hurts of life we experience. So when we talk with God, He understands! You and I need to run to Him when we experience the hurts of life.

At the very least, we need to be praying for the hurting person. Ask God to comfort them. Ask that they would feel His presence. Ask Him for direction for you as well as next steps for the wounded person.

When Erica received that disappointing letter, we lavished love on her, listened to her talk about her disappointment, let her grieve the loss, and eventually talked about her educational options. Most importantly, though, we prayed with her and for her. We didn't really know what the next step was, but we knew the One who knew the next step. And that's the power of prayer.

Emotional Intimacy Is the Goal

Erica is now on the other side of her school disappointment. She had gone to a small Christian school from second grade to eighth grade and had been one of about 14 in her class. Had she gone to U-High as she had dreamed, she would have been in a class of 150 students. However, as she began her freshman year at Normal Community High School, she found herself in a class of 500. It was overwhelming.

The first two weeks of school were emotionally exhausting for her. She knew no one and found herself eating lunch alone every day. That's the end of the world for a freshman girl! She came home in tears almost every day those first few weeks. On the third day she came home and said she was overwhelmed with all the food options at lunch. There were a half-dozen different lines with so many meal options that she couldn't figure out what line to get in to get whatever food was offered. Each afternoon I listened to her fears and frustrations and encouraged her as best I could. That day I knew I needed to take action. I asked Erica to jump in the car and we drove right over to the school. We walked into the guidance office and found her academic advisor, who I kindly asked to give us an after-hours tour of the lunchroom. She gladly accommodated our request and walked us through the empty lunchroom, explaining the lunch options available in each line. It was an absolute relief for Erica to have these explanations given to her in a nonthreatening atmosphere.

Erica and I grew closer in our relationship through this difficult season of her life. She talked, I listened. She cried, I comforted. We prayed together. I grew to know her better, and in time she got to know me better. Now we're over a year out from that experience, and Erica can't imagine being anywhere else. She now realizes the unique opportunities she has had and will have in this school. She has grown in character through the experience, and we have grown in intimacy as a family.

Whether it's a husband who has lost a job or a teenager dealing with the loss of their first love, when home is a well-functioning trauma unit, emotional intimacy deepens. One of the best definitions of intimacy I've ever heard is "in to me see." Intimacy is experienced when we let others see into our heart. It happens when we share our burdens with one another. And when we feel safe to share our inner life and are encouraged to do so, we are setting a foundation of intimacy in relationships for life.

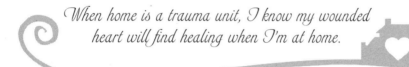

When home is a trauma unit, I know my wounded heart will find healing when I'm at home.

4

Home as a Church

Faith is a constant thread strengthening the fabric of our family.

THOMAS KINKADE

Between birth and age 18, a parent will spend approximately 58,200 waking hours with their child. If the family takes that child to church for two hours every week during the same period of time, the church will have the child for just 1872 hours. With that disparity in hours of influence, why do we as parents often leave it to the church to be our child's primary spiritual influence?

The home is the number one place for spiritual knowledge to be passed on. Too often, however, we are passive in our responsibility to spiritually train our children. Our passivity is usually fueled by a lack of knowledge of where to begin. If we want our children to embrace faith for their own life, we have to realize that they have to see a relationship with Christ as a priority in our life.

Do as I Do

A parent's actions will speak far louder than their words. If we tell our children God wants us to tell the truth, but then ask them to tell a salesperson on the phone that we're not home when we're standing right there in the kitchen, we've completely undone our teaching. Parenting with an attitude of "do as I say, not as I do" reeks of hypocrisy and proves to be an ineffective way to parent. C. Lenox Redmond said, "Judicious mothers will always keep in mind that they are the first book read, and the last put aside, in every child's library."

I used to become frustrated when my kids would get up early from their nap and interrupt my quiet time with the Lord. But soon I realized that it was one of the most effective ways to teach them about spending time with God. Instead of trying to get them back to sleep, I would gently pull them on my lap and read aloud from the Bible or include them in my prayer time.

One mom I know found she could have a better quiet time at a local restaurant. She told her two teen boys that she would buy them breakfast out each morning if they would like to accompany her and have their own quiet time. Now those boys are young men with a firm foundation of faith.

If you've never spent much time in the Bible or praying, I think you'll be surprised at the vision, hope, and perspective you'll find when you keep your eye on the Mountain Mover (God) rather than the mountains in your life. If reading the Bible is new for you, a great place to start is in the book of Proverbs. There are 31 chapters in Proverbs and many months have 31 days—by reading the chapter in Proverbs that corresponds with the day of the month, you'll make it through the book of Proverbs each month. This is a great way to help your kids start reading their Bible too.

After you get started reading regularly, you might go to Matthew, Mark, Luke, or John. These books tell the story of the life of Jesus Christ, and they are packed full of God's principles for how we are to live.

When home is a church, Mom and Dad are the pastors. Because of that, Mom and Dad need to live a life of integrity. The best place to start doing that is in our own personal relationship with Jesus Christ.

Say Yes!

I was raised in church all of my life; however, it wasn't until I was 19 years old that I wholeheartedly said yes to Jesus Christ. That's when I moved from religion to relationship and a whole new quality of life opened up for me.

I decided to get involved with the Greek system at Butler University when I pledged Alpha Chi Omega and moved into the sorority house within the first few weeks of my freshman year of school. One of my sorority sisters, Beth, introduced me to contemporary Christian music. Beth and I would sit at the piano in the living room of our house singing the music of Amy Grant, Keith Green, and others. The words of the songs introduced me to a very real God. He wasn't far away and formal as I had known Him; He was intimate, loving, and a friend the like of which I'd never known.

God used that freshman year in college to soften my heart toward Him. He watered the seeds of faith that had been planted in my childhood church and planted new seeds of truth through Beth and others I met. I said yes to God and then said yes to Mark when he asked me to marry him. We became engaged in November and married June 25—just six weeks after I finished my first year of college. After we were married, we found a church home where we began to deepen our faith and both made the decision to be baptized as adults.

I have a rich heritage of faith from my years of being raised in the church. I was baptized as an infant and went through confirmation when I was in junior high. I also participated in many years of Sunday school, youth group, and church camp. God used all of those experiences to prepare me for a lifelong relationship with Him. However, my faith didn't become fully real to me until it was solely my decision, my surrendered yes to God. It was then that it moved from "going to church" (religion) to "knowing and following God" (relationship).

Have you said yes to God? Are you even aware that He's offered you a relationship that will not only determine where you'll spend eternity, but also enrich the quality of your life in more ways than you could ever imagine? Are you aware that Jesus Christ hand-delivered your invitation when He went to the cross for you and me? Now you and I sit with a personalized invitation to God's party in heaven, and He's just waiting for us to RSVP.

If you've never said yes to God, don't toss the invitation aside.

Respond today. Tell Him that you accept His invitation and want to know more. You can do this by talking to God and saying something like this: *"God, I want to know You more. I don't want religion in my life; I want relationship. Thank You for sending Your Son, Jesus, to die on the cross for me. This is the day I say 'yes' to You and accept You as my Savior."* This is such an essential step of faith, because when Mom and Dad live life in relationship with Jesus Christ, it paves the way for their home to become the church it was meant to be.

Tell the Stories

Jesus taught many life principles by telling stories people could relate to. He would take a common life situation and apply a godly principle to it. People understood it because it applied to their life. The Bible calls these stories "parables," and they set a pattern for us as parents to follow as we teach our children godly principles.

One night as my boys were brushing their teeth before bed, I grabbed a paper plate and asked them to each squeeze a big blob of toothpaste onto it. They thought that was great fun. Then I asked them to put the toothpaste back into the tube. Of course, they couldn't do that. Then I shared that this was an important picture to remember because that toothpaste is just like our words. When mean words come out of our mouth, we can't take them back. They leave our lips and do their damage right away. Then I shared with them that there is a verse in the Bible that says "Do not let any unwholesome talk come out of your mouths, but only what is helpful for building others up according to their needs" (Ephesians 4:29). Finally, I asked them to remember that truth every time they brushed their teeth.

That was a parable made for a child. It wasn't a formal teaching. It wasn't sitting around a table saying, "Now, children, we're going to have our devotional lesson for the day." It was simply inserted right into the daily routine of life. I can't take credit for coming up with the toothpaste analogy—I had read it somewhere in a book. All I did was watch for a teachable moment and then capitalized on it to the fullest.

The best strategy for us to pass on the foundations of faith is to look for teachable moments. When those moments present themselves, we can share God's truth in such a way that our children can best understand it. There are great resources for parents to find similar life lessons. You might start with www.famtime.com.

A Family That Prays Together Stays Together

Anne called me from college in tears. Something had happened on campus, and she was struggling with intense fear and a loss of her sense of security in the environment in which she was living. She happened to catch me on my cell phone while I was shopping. I stood out in the middle of the mall listening to her concerns and fears. As much as I wanted to, there wasn't anything I could do about the situation other than reassure her. This was one of those times in life where she was going to have to muster up courage and lean into God's truth for herself.

After listening to her and asking her some questions, I finally said to her, "Anne, I don't know what to do to help you through this, but I know the One who has the answer. Let's pray for direction." There I stood, right outside of Bath and Body Works, praying with my 19-year-old daughter on the phone about a very real fear she was experiencing in her life.

Praying together wasn't something we always did as a family. In my early years of mothering, I parented very much the way I was raised—praying with my kids primarily at dinnertime and bedtime. However, as I grew in my faith, I knew I wanted something more for my kids. When Anne and Evan were in late elementary school, I decided I wanted prayer to be more than something we did as a routine of life. I wanted it to be part of the fabric of our family. I wanted us to consider it normal to pray about anything anytime of the day.

I had to learn to do that first, and I began by talking to God throughout my day. I learned that prayer can happen in a variety of ways. Sometimes we can sit down and have an extended prayer time, which is just like having a nice, long meal with a friend. Sometimes we can have a brief chat with God while we're driving somewhere or standing at the park swinging our kids, which is more like having a snack with Him. And then other times we make a request for a quick dose of wisdom—I call these arrow prayers. They are like shooting up an arrow to God with a single question in mind, such as, "What do I do here, Lord?"

As I began to make conversation with God a normal part of my day, it became easier to introduce my children to the concept of talking to Him anytime. We started slowly. When they would have a decision to make, I would talk through their options with them, but then I would say, "Let's ask God what He wants you to do. I'm sure He'll give you a sense of peace one way or the other." Then we would pray together right there—standing in the kitchen or riding in the car. Let me tell you, that was a stretch for me; I'd never seen it done before. It was something I could envision but didn't know quite how to walk it out. This was a new path I was paving and, honestly, it felt awkward in the beginning. However, in time, it became a part of who we are as a family. We pushed through the awkward feeling of doing something new, and now it's so natural for our family to pray together that I can't imagine it any other way.

A Neighborhood Influence

Most churches consider the influence they have on the community around them. They often have specific events, such as Vacation Bible School or special Christmas programs, that reach out to those who might not regularly attend church. When home is a church, you have the opportunity to shine a light into a dark world.

Children from unstable homes will be drawn to the stability of a home filled with God's love. Seeds of truth, hope, and acceptance can be planted in the fertile soil of a young life when your "church" reaches out to those who live nearby. Several years ago we featured a drama at our Hearts at Home conferences called "The Lemonade Mom." The drama started with a man who was being given an award for his life accomplishments. In his acknowledgments, he named a person who had been a huge influence in his life. His influencer then shared with the audience his story and how he had been influenced by someone else. The pattern continued through several people until you saw where the influence began—the final character remembered a woman who served as his primary influence in life. She wasn't a coach or a teacher. She was a mom—a mom in the neighborhood in which he grew up. The man spoke about the influence this woman had on him—he called her "The Lemonade Mom"—as she had routinely served lemonade at her kitchen table and listened to him, accepted him, directed him, and loved him throughout his growing up years.

Many families have made their home a church and neighborhood influence by hosting a "backyard Bible club," where they serve snacks and share a puppet show or craft project that allows for the seeds of God's truth to be planted in a child's heart. Other families have found that simply offering a ride to church and Sunday school to a child whose family doesn't attend church can open the door for a lifetime relationship with Christ. Still others just make their home a hangout place for their kids' friends. They plant seeds by being available, loving, and encouraging the youth each time they are in their home.

Maybe the influence you have is on the moms and dads in the neighborhood. One couple I know hosts a neighborhood volleyball match once a week throughout the summer with the goal of building relationship that can someday turn into spiritual influence. You might have a moms night out once a month to build relationship and plant seeds of influence.

A Lifestyle of Faith

Christianity is more than just going to church—it's a way of life. It starts with our lives and hearts and transfers to our children's lives and hearts. When we know we need to teach our kids, we learn more ourselves. When we learn more ourselves, our faith deepens. It's a win-win situation for everyone involved.

Religion is compartmentalized into a portion of our life, while relationship permeates every aspect of our lives. Kids want authenticity in a parent's spiritual life. This gives them something to model, follow after, and eventually embrace as their own. Authenticity happens when we live a lifestyle of faith that comes out of a loving relationship with a living God.

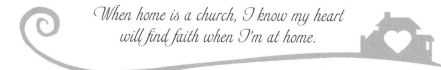

When home is a church, I know my heart will find faith when I'm at home.

PART II
The Framework

5

Home as a Pep Rally

A family's love makes a house a home.

THOMAS KINKADE

Erica was playing her best game ever. Her serves were strong and she was playing offense and defense equally well. Because of that her volleyball coach was giving her a lot of playing time. It was a good night, and not only were Mark and I there to encourage her, but her four siblings were there as well. She had her own fan club and cheering section!

Every home has the ability to serve as a pep rally for each member of the family. It's a place where we are celebrated, encouraged, and cheered on. It's a place to know one another and be known. It's a place of safety and unconditional love. Home needs to be a place where our potential is realized and where the message is loud and clear, "We believe in you and all God has in store for you!"

Just living under one roof, however, doesn't guarantee a pep rally environment. A family of five can be living five very individual lives with everyone heading in different directions every day. Or the same family can live life in community with one another, cheering one another on.

In order for home to serve as an ongoing pep rally, we have to intentionally create an atmosphere of encouragement and celebration. Let's look at some principles to make that happen.

Celebrate the Ordinary

Does Johnny have a soccer game on Saturday? Any family member who is home heads to the game to cheer him on. Is Susie singing in a school choir concert? Gather the troops to attend the concert together with a trip for ice cream afterward. As your children get into grade school, have a discussion about the importance of celebrating one another. Set the standard that all family members will attend one another's events unless they have something else going on at the same time. This creates a ready-made cheering section and pep rally for each member of the family.

Another way to celebrate the ordinary is to create traditions or keep your eyes open for random celebrations. Is it Monday? If so, it's "special dessert" night. Is it snowing outside? Then it's time for snow ice cream!

Holly Schurter, a mother of eight, describes the concept of celebrating the ordinary in her Hearts at Home article:

> Children love to celebrate. And celebrations—as well as the happy memories they create—cement healthy, loving family relationships.
>
> There is more to celebrate with our children than the "big" holidays. Our culture bombards us with ideas for celebrations from New Year's Eve and Valentine's Day right through Thanksgiving and Christmas, and everything the calendar displays in between.
>
> Most of us are careful to pick and choose the ideas that fit our family's rituals, traditions, and budget even as we try to make those celebrations fun and meaningful for our children. But no calendar alerts us ahead of time to the everyday celebrations that happen when someone gets an especially good grade on an essay or passes a difficult math test. No one warns us when the first crocuses will bloom or the first snowflakes will fall so we can plan a party. The trick is to be ready for such serendipitous celebrations.
>
> At our house, at the very back of the tea and coffee shelf is the "party pantry." There we keep a tin of special tea, a bag of flavored coffee, some packets of cocoa, a bag of jelly beans or cookies— scrumptious, we-don't-eat-this-every-day treats to be pulled out in the event of a sudden celebration.

In the dining room, the sideboard has a drawer with nothing but color-ful napkins, some fragrant candles, and a few surprises—like bottles of bubbles to blow at each other across the dining room table.

Still, it isn't the supplies that make the celebration. It's the way we open our hearts to life's lovely surprises, those everyday things worth celebrating. We watch for the first snowfall; it calls for cocoa around the fireplace as surely as a birthday party at school calls for cupcakes. A good report card means dinner out to celebrate, while bubbles at the breakfast table could mean anything from crocuses in the backyard to the great speech someone gave at school yesterday.

Nearly every day of our lives offers some good and perfect gift to cel-ebrate. The trick is to recognize the gift and be ready to celebrate.[1]

I believe Holly captures the essence of celebrating the ordinary. She has created for her family a pep rally environment where they not only celebrate one another, but they celebrate life in general. The next time you see colored napkins on sale or little bottles of celebration bubbles at the dollar store, pick them up and tuck them away to be ready to celebrate the ordinary.

Celebrate Rites of Passage

Both Anne and Heather celebrated their thirteenth birthdays within days of one another. Anne is our oldest daughter and Heather is my friend Julie's oldest daughter. Julie and I planned a special mother-daughter trip with our girls to celebrate this rite of passage into the teen years. We whisked the girls away for a weekend of shopping, pampering, and special time to talk with them about the young women they were becoming.

When each of our children turn 11, their Aunt Juli and Uncle Kyle spend an entire day with them doing whatever activity they desire. Each of our children has counted down the days until their eleventh birthday, anticipating the special celebration of this stage in their life.

It's important that families celebrate rites of passage. Important transitions in a child's life include puberty, school changes (that is, moving from elementary school to junior high), a first job, and getting a driver's license. We need to affirm that indeed these are important milestones in their life. In the movie *Cheaper by the Dozen 2,* the mother of 12 children shares this wisdom, "Letting go is the hardest thing to do: You have to settle in the past, engage in the present, and believe in the future." Rites of passage not only allow children to celebrate a stage in their life, but they also help us let go as we settle in the past, engage in the present, and believe in the future.

What happens if parents don't pay attention to the rites of passage in their children's lives? Unfortunately kids will often go out and make up their own rites of passage. This is where the allure of sexual experimentation or alcohol or drug usage becomes a draw. Kids want to celebrate their independence in ways that are not only readily available in teen culture, but also incredibly destructive to their lives.

If you've never discussed celebrating rites of passage with your spouse, start by talking about how they were handled in the home you were each raised in. Make note of traditions that would be valuable to carry on. Then list the rites of passage you would like to celebrate as a family and brainstorm ideas to celebrate those life transitions. Don't let the business of life squeeze out celebrating rites of passage. This is an important element in a pep rally environment.

Celebrate Birthdays

At the Savage household, birthdays are a special event. While the birthday person sleeps on the night before their birthday, Mom and Dad sneak in and decorate their room and doorway with balloons and streamers. We also set the dining room table with birthday plates and napkins, and decorate the birthday person's chair with streamers and balloons.

When the birthday person awakes in the morning, he opens his eyes to a decorated room that immediately proclaims the message that today is his special day. When he heads downstairs there are more decorations, and one of the best parts of the day: cake and ice cream for breakfast! We gather as a family, give him his gifts and cards, and launch into a day that celebrates his life and special day.

Our limited family budget has never allowed for extravagant birthday presents, but I don't believe our children have ever felt they missed much. Our celebrations speak love and value to the birthday person—something a gift of any size could never do nearly as well.

Find some special traditions that match the personality of your family and make them a part of your birthday celebrations. One family I know takes the birthday person to their favorite restaurant for dinner. Another family might make the birthday person's favorite meal at home. You might have a tradition of telling the story of the birthday person's actual birth, or pull out family videos or scrapbooks that chronicle their life.

When we celebrate our adopted son's birthday, we pull out the videos we took of the orphanage where he spent the first nine years of his life—it's his favorite video to watch. We sometimes look at the one lone childhood picture we have of him, a black-and-white picture of a pouty-faced 18-month-old, and muse with him about what might have made him have such a somber look on his face. Sometimes he wants to talk about what he imagines his birth parents to be like or what they would have done on the day he was born. The important thing is that we celebrate his life—the parts we weren't a part of and the parts we have been a part of. It's our day to focus on him—and no one else—so that he knows how important he is as a person and as a member of our family.

Celebrate Accomplishments

On the day that Erica learned she had made the school musical, I set the "It's Your Special Day" dinner plate at her place at the table. On the day that Kolya made a goal during his soccer game, I set it at his place. Everyone needs to know they have friends and family who can celebrate with them when they've done something well.

When our children were young, we worked with them to be good sports when playing board games. If they were the loser, they needed to be able to help celebrate the winner. Rather than sulk after losing, we had them give a high five to their brother or sister and congratulate them on their accomplishment. This fostered an environment of encouragement rather than competition.

As parents we need to keep an eye on how to keep celebrating accomplishments balanced within the family. You might have one child that excels at anything he puts his mind to and another who struggles to do well. If you're not careful, you'll naturally be giving more encouragement to the child who excels at sports, gets good grades, or tries out and makes every school musical, while another child is content to sit at home reading books or managing their own babysitting service. Accomplishments need to be individualized to accommodate each person's temperament, personality, and abilities.

Celebrate Individuality

God has wired each one of us differently. Many times those differences frustrate us. However, when home is a pep rally, we need to turn those frustrations into fascination. Does one child excel in math and another in history? Show them how to help one another in their area of strength. Is one child a thinker and another a feeler? Rather than allowing them to criticize one another because they process life differently, help them to see the benefits of each other's personalities. The thinker may think through options well when making decisions. If so, tap into their ability to think through and weigh options when you need to make a decision. Thank them for their help in processing the options. Encourage their siblings to seek them out when they need to make big decisions. The feeler may have a lot of compassion for others. When sorting through a relational issue, the feeler can help you empathize with the other person or consider how they might be feeling or thinking. Encourage siblings to trust the intuition their feeling brother or sister might offer.

Many times we handle differences within the family by teasing others about their differences. This is when home becomes more like a target range than a pep rally. As parents we need to model celebrating each other's differences and refrain from seeing those differences as wrong. We need to have zero tolerance for sibling rivalry and make sibling revelry the standard for the family.

Encourage Effort

Austin and Kolya were on an undefeated soccer team. The last game of the season, however, they met their match. The opposing team was also undefeated, and they soon took the lead and eventually won the game. Even in the face of certain loss, our team continued to play with excellence. The boys fought hard and kept their heads in the game until the end. The coach later told us that when they huddled before the last quarter, one of the boys said, "Let's make our goal this quarter to not let them score at all." The boys rallied around that vision—there was no way they could win, but they could work to keep the opposing team from scoring more points. And they did! When it was all over, we told the boys that though they might not have won the game, they won in determination and sportsmanship. We wanted to not only celebrate accomplishment, but also encourage incredible effort.

Many of us have heard the saying, "It doesn't matter if you lose or win; it's how you play the game." Most of us would agree with that statement, but sometimes our actions don't match the value. For instance, do you take your child out for ice cream primarily when their team wins, or do you do it when they lose the game but played well? Do you only put "A" papers on the refrigerator, or would you post a "C" paper when you know they worked hard on the project and did their best?

We need to recognize the effort our children make. If you are working on having your child make their bed well, celebrate improvement, even if the completed task is still not up to your standards. Many of us are such perfectionists that anything less than perfect is grounds for criticism or correction. When children live in "perfectionistic" environments where there seems to be no chance they will be celebrated unless they are perfect, they either lack determination because they've learned they can't win or they become people pleasers trying to earn the recognition, and ultimately love, they long for.

Encourage Dreams

Are you a dream maker or dream taker when it comes to your spouse and your kids? This is a question I've had to ask myself many times over the years. My practical, black-and-white thinking doesn't leave much space for dreaming. However, I've learned that many times I take my family member's dreams away rather than making their dreams come true. If at all possible, you and I need to partner with the lofty goals of those we love.

Our ten-year-old son, Austin, has a tender heart. When his older brother and sister traveled to Jamaica on a youth group mission trip, Austin announced that he wanted to do a sword-throwing show to raise money for the mission team's work projects. Every day he took his plastic toy swords out in the yard and worked up a routine to music. Soon he wanted to print up invitations to give to people at church to come to his show. I couldn't imagine that this endeavor would be successful, and every part of me wanted to discourage Austin in this "foolish" event. I refrained, however, realizing that I needed to be a dream maker, not a dream taker. And God blessed both my obedience and Austin's efforts when more than 15 people came to his show. Between the ticket price and donations accepted at the door, he earned more than $100 for the special project! (Thank You, God, for helping me get it right this time.)

When our children dream, we need to dream along with them. If necessary, we can gently lead them to discover just how feasible their dream might really be. When our 19-year-old son was finishing up his freshman year of college, he and a friend began dreaming about renting an apartment together over the summer. I knew his dreams didn't match his pocketbook, but instead of telling him how foolish his idea was, I encouraged him to begin checking out apartments. His dad and I sat with him and made a list of living expenses he would incur living on his own. When he looked at the realities of his dream, he soon realized it wasn't really feasible. He was disappointed but not damaged in the process.

When we are dream makers rather than dream takers, we celebrate the ideas, hopes, and dreams of our family members, even if we have to take the long road to help them either accomplish their dreams or do the research to see if they are even reachable goals to have.

A Pep Club for Life

When I was in high school, I was a part of the pep club and the pep band. The pep club sat together and worked with the cheerleaders to excite the crowd and encourage the team. The pep band played at all the basketball games, adding excitement to the game environment. During the school year we held regular pep rallies to cheer on the players and elevate school spirit. Our home can serve our family in the same way as we cheer one another on and increase our family spirit in the game of life.

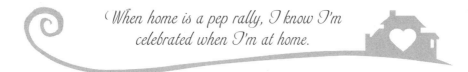

When home is a pep rally, I know I'm celebrated when I'm at home.

~ 6 ~

Home as a Research Lab

When parents do too much for their children, their
children do too little for themselves.

ELBERT HUBBARD

W here did you learn to cook?" I asked Jim, who is a chef at a
popular local restaurant. "At home. From the time I could
stand on a stool in the kitchen and work with my mom." Jim's
mom understood the value of giving her children opportunities. She
could have shooed him out of the kitchen, discouraging his culinary
interest. Instead she noted his curiosity and let him participate as
he was able.

Home is a safe place to develop new skills, try new hobbies,
and cultivate ideas. It's a place where talents can be developed and
honed. Home needs to be a place to discover not only what we
like to do, but also what we don't enjoy or have little talent for at
all. Jim's interest in the kitchen began at an early age. Few young
children will show an interest in something that will become their
career someday. For the most part, kids need the opportunity to try
many activities to discern their skill and interest. When home is a
research lab, it provides the perfect place for self-discovery.

In the Kitchen

We all need to learn some basic life skills, regardless of what we will
choose as our vocation. Children need a variety of food preparation

opportunities throughout childhood and adolescence. It takes time
to show them how to peel a carrot or potato, but it gives them
ownership of the meal and introduces them to basic culinary skills.
You never know what God has in store for your child.

Require regular help in the kitchen by every child, but give extra
opportunities to any child who shows more interest. At an early
age children can help wash fruits and vegetables. For the child who
wants to do more, allow them to help make one part of the meal.
Dessert is a great place to begin.

Instant pudding is a dessert that can be used in a variety of
ways. First children learn to measure and mix the pudding. Then
they can fill dessert dishes and place them in the refrigerator. Later
on after the meal they can add a dollop of whipped topping and
serve them to the family. After they have the basic "how to" down
for pudding, they can get creative. If they make a box of chocolate
pudding in one bowl and a box of vanilla pudding in another bowl,
they can layer the two puddings in parfait glasses. What a beautiful
dessert that makes, and what a sense of accomplishment it gives to
a young cook. With the help of a graham cracker piecrust, they can
also follow the instructions for pie filling and make a refrigerated
pie for dinner.

After some basic desserts have been mastered, they can make
eggs for breakfast, grilled cheese sandwiches for lunch, and breaded
chicken breasts for dinner. These will begin to give foundational
knowledge of food preparation and let them become knowledgeable
of the culinary arts.

If an interest grows, give opportunity outside the home whenever
possible. Sign up for food, cake decorating, or some other area of
interest at your local 4-H club. Check out opportunities to shadow
a chef for a day or take a summer cooking class. Eventually you can
encourage them to get a food service job, which further exposes
them to food preparation or management as a career possibility.

In the Garage
Jeff's dad told Jeff the engine in the garage was his very own.

He could dismantle it, use parts from it, or explore it in any way he wanted to. Jeff was interested in mechanics, and his dad wanted to give him an opportunity to explore. Jennifer's dad did the same thing with an old computer. Rather than discarding it, he saw an opportunity to let Jennifer expand her technical mind. Many kids learn best with hands-on kinesthetic learning. If you have a kinesthetic learner, providing opportunity to tear something apart and put it back together will excite them more than a trip to McDonald's, and it will whet their appetite to learn.

Kids need two things from us to make this happen: permission and space. Most kinesthetic learning brings about some level of a mess. They need permission to make the mess and a designated space to do so. Give them their opportunities and boundaries at the same time so they are clear on the space they can use, the tools they have access to, and the responsibilities they have for cleanup. Encourage them by showing an interest in what they are learning and applauding their efforts.

If you have to take the car to the auto shop, have your mechanic-in-training accompany you to drop the car off and talk with the mechanic. If you have a technically savvy friend working on your computer, ask them if they could allow your son or daughter to help with the repair or upgrade. Who knows what might come of such opportunities? Your own child might build your next computer or have the ability to fix your car when it breaks down.

In the Yard

Got a child with a green thumb? Someone interested in agriculture or landscaping? Every child needs some basic skills in taking care of a yard or growing plants, but there might be a budding horticulturist in your family.

Every spring I plant about a dozen pots of flowers for our porch and deck. It's a job I never do alone. I always ask the kids to assist me in preparing the soil and transplanting the flowers into the pots. Erica loves to help design the color scheme for each pot—it puts her designing skills to work. The boys enjoy digging and getting dirty, so they are happy to oblige.

If your family has a garden, make caring for it a family affair. As a child, I remember our family gardening together every summer. We all helped plant, weed, and harvest the crops. We also learned to can and freeze fruits and vegetables so we would have them year-round. My two sisters and I didn't take that research any further than that experience, but we have the skill and knowledge to garden as adults if we so desire.

In the Library

Do you have a reader in the house? Reading is a skill that will bring pleasure for a lifetime. A child with a love of words will most likely be a lifetime learner. They may even take their love of the written language into a career in the publishing industry as a writer or editor. They may choose to teach English, write plays, or craft speeches. To challenge the avid reader, check out *www.wikipedia.com*, where you'll find an online library and encyclopedia that satisfies the appetite of anyone who loves words.

What if you have a child who doesn't enjoy reading? Should you still encourage them to read? Absolutely! You'll just have to work a little harder to find something they're interested in. I have two children who love to read and three that could take it or leave it. My book lovers rarely have to be guided to reading material. They seek it out for themselves and always have something they're reading. My other three, however, need encouragement and suggestions for titles that might interest them. Usually it takes more than a half-dozen suggestions before I find the right one that piques their interest. Use the summer reading program at the library, book order forms that come home from the school, and even a walk down the book aisle at Wal-Mart to acquaint your less-than-enthusiastic reader with all the options available. Don't forget that magazines, comic books, and other types of periodicals count as reading too. As with any other media, our children need our guidance on appropriate reading materials. Don't look the other way if your child picks up a book or magazine that doesn't match your family's standards or isn't age appropriate for them. Guide them to a choice that matches your standards, piques their interest, and meets their reading ability.

In the Office

Some kids are born entrepreneurs. They can take a concept from creation to completion with little effort. They are born leaders who aren't afraid of taking a risk or trying something new.

Scouting programs, student council, or even serving as a page in the state legislature provide opportunities to develop leadership skills, try new environments, and see a variety of uses for the gift of leadership.

Leaders often become business owners. They identify a community need that matches their knowledge and skills, and they take the risk to develop their idea. When home is a research lab, it encourages an entrepreneurial spirit in a child. A successful lab says "You can do it!" and "I believe in you!"

Our 12-year-old son, Kolya, has created his own car cleaning business. He calls it Kolya's Kustom Kar Kleaning. He made advertising flyers on the computer and handed them out to people at church. He's a hard worker, and his reputation of doing a great job has earned him new customers. He sets up appointments for people and works to make his customers happy, cleaning both the inside and outside of their vehicle. When he asked about "formalizing" his business, Mark and I weren't sure he could really make it happen, but we wanted to be dream makers rather than dream takers, so we came alongside him and helped him accomplish his goal. Now he's earning income with his unique, self-created business.

In the Arena

Participation in sports helps children not only stay in good physical shape, but also may go as far as providing partial or full college scholarships one day. And someone's child has to play in the NFL or the Major or Minor Baseball Leagues or even compete in the Olympics, although those are certainly extraordinary, but possible, experiences too.

A sports parent has to recognize other authority figures in their child's life. There is nothing more frustrating to a child than to be given instructions on a baseball field from both his coach and his yelling parents on the sidelines. As hard as it is, the most important thing we can communicate during a game is encouragement. Kids need Mom and Dad to pitch them balls or give them occasional tips before or after a game, but they don't need them to act as if they are managing a future Major League baseball career. You and I need to be parents first and let the coaches do the coaching.

In the grade school years, kids have many opportunities to try out a variety of sports. It's important, however, to remember the whole concept of margin when making decisions about what sports your kids will or won't do and at what age they'll start. A stressed-out child won't excel at any sport.

Any parent whose child is interested in sports ought to invest in some comfortable lawn chairs and bleacher cushions. A lot of sitting out in the elements happens when your research lab includes sporting events.

In the Conservatory

Our son Evan is a musician. He is an accomplished songwriter, vocalist, guitarist, and pianist. Evan loves to sit in the living room playing and writing his music for hours. But don't ask him to use his voice in a musical theater setting. One stint in the chorus of his high school production of *Fiddler on the Roof* was all it took for Evan to say, "That's not for me!" He enjoys watching musical theater, but he doesn't enjoy participating in it. His younger sister is exactly the opposite. Erica loves the stage! Give her a musical audition, and she's on the front row waiting to try out.

There's no failure in finding out what you like and don't like. There's also no failure in figuring out that something doesn't really come natural to you. All of our kids have taken piano lessons—that's a nonnegotiable for their piano teacher mother. However, it was very obvious that while our oldest daughter, Anne, has a beautiful singing voice and loves vocal music, piano never came easily to her. After several years of lessons, she asked if she could invest her time elsewhere. Her father and I applauded her efforts and told her that her basic piano knowledge would serve her well as a singer, and then we let her stop the lessons.

Erica and Evan, on the other hand, have taken to piano like fish take to water. They both had their moments of wanting to quit, but I knew that was part of the challenge of staying committed to something over the long haul. During those times we reignited their interest by conferring with the teacher about playing some styles of music they each loved. Erica stays interested by playing one "movie theme" piece and one classical piece at all times. Evan is now in college and beyond the piano lessons stage of life. He is studying music business and hopes to be a studio musician or musical artist someday. His experiences in the research lab helped to both know what he didn't want to do (Broadway) and what he loves to do (anything in the commercial music business).

Anytime a child begins to explore music, a parent should invest in a very good pair of earplugs. (Just kidding—well, actually, I am half serious.) Musical skill is acquired only through practice and the making of many mistakes. Any band or orchestra instrument first sounds like the mating call of a dying goose or something more akin to fingernails scratching on a chalkboard. It takes time for a child to successfully make music. It is essential during this time, however, that they receive lots of encouragement from you. Applaud them when you faintly recognize "Yankee Doodle Dandy" or "My Wild Irish Rose." Reward good attitudes and good practice routines. Once they begin to get the hang of the instrument, you can pick up a beginner's book of popular music (movie themes, Broadway musicals, etc.) to complement what they are playing for school or lessons and keep them interested in their instrument.

If true skill and an honest desire to learn the instrument ensue, private lessons can take the research to a new level. A music student is almost assured of improving his skill with individualized instruction. Regardless of how far a student goes musically, any musical experience or skills will enrich a child's life in one way or another.

Our two fifth graders just began their band experience. Austin has decided to pursue trumpet and Kolya has chosen trombone. I think I'm bypassing the earplugs and heading straight for the soundproof headphones.

The Chameleon Parent

Erica loves to shop. I hate to shop. Erica has an eye for fashion and has considered fashion design as a career possibility for herself. I, on the other hand, am a creature of habit. I don't need new clothes because there is nothing wrong with the ones I have. I have little need for fashion.

Erica's love for fashion has taught me that I need to be interested in the things my kids are interested in. If they love football, I'd better learn what offside means. If they love art, I need to know the different mediums they might use (sculpture, oil-based or watercolor painting, etc.) regardless of whether I can draw a decent stick person or not. In Erica's case, I've had to learn to love shopping. Honestly, she's content to go to the mall and not spend a dime. She just wants to see the clothing styles, sometimes examining how a piece of clothing is made or how an outfit is assembled on a mannequin. I have learned to find joy in a trip to the mall—not because I love shopping—but because I love Erica.

If you have a child who shows an interest in something you have no interest in, ask God to show you how to step into their world. Resist the temptation to discourage an interest you see leading to no career or moneymaking value. Remember that boys may be interested in something (like cooking) that you might consider a female interest. And girls may want to step into something (like auto mechanics) that you might not consider very ladylike. This needs to also be acceptable. The skills and experience they gain in your research lab may be just the first or second step in ten or twelve that will eventually lead them to discover what they want to do as a career or vocation.

You and I have to learn to be a chameleon parent—changing our color to match the color of our child's interest. If we are successful, each child will feel they have a personal cheering section for whatever skill they try or subject matter they show interest in.

Lifelong Knowledge

When I was in junior high, I attended two years of a summer exploratory program at a local school. I tried my hand at floral designing, television producing, fabricating plastics, woodworking, and more. The classes available to me were limitless, and my parents encouraged me to explore whatever interested me. While I didn't end up choosing a career in any of the areas I explored over those two summers, I still pull from the knowledge I gained in the learning process. I know how to use basic woodworking tools, and that plastics class gave me some basic knowledge when I married a man whose family owned a plastics business. The basic elements I learned in floral designing I still use when I place flowers from the yard in a vase. I learned the basics of making boutonnieres and corsages, and I put that to use this summer when we prepared for our daughter's wedding.

Anytime a person can gain knowledge, it is never a waste of time. That knowledge will both expand their mind and help narrow their vocational and career choices as they experience the options available. Furthermore, it grows in them an "I can do it!" attitude. In the words of Thomas Kinkade, "When I think back to my own childhood days, the words that seem to fill my memories and epitomize my childhood are: 'Let's do it.' I'm convinced there's something in that 'let's do it now' mentality that is a vital secret to childlike joy. There's something inherently joyous about being able to think of something great to do and then jump into the idea with both bare feet."

Kids need many opportunities to jump into ideas with both bare feet. They need to try on different skills to see what fits them best. When we help them do it, it feels like a vote of confidence in their potential. And when someone believes in you, you can't help but believe in yourself and all that God has in store for you.

When home is a research lab, I know I will encounter possibilities when I'm at home.

7

Home as a School

*A family is a place where principles are hammered
and honed on the anvil of everyday living.*

CHUCK SWINDOLL

"Mom, you forgot to tell us about the tollbooths!" my 17-year-old son exclaimed to me upon his return home from his first road trip to Chicago with three friends. "Oh, Evan. I'm so sorry. I completely forgot you'd be driving on a tollway." I replied. "We were so scared when we came up on the first one, Mom, because we didn't have the right change. It was a 40-cent toll, but we only had 50 cents. We held our breath as we threw the money in, hoping the traffic arm would go up and let us through." His words were tumbling out faster than I could keep up with him. "Then the same thing happened at the next one too, and we worried whether it would let us through." "Evan," I responded when I could get a word in edgewise, "when you don't have the right change, you don't use the automatic lanes. That's when you use the manual lanes so you don't overpay the toll." "Well, Mom, we know that now," he replied rather sheepishly. "It wasn't until the third toll booth that we all figured out that the words 'automatic' and 'manual' didn't refer to the type of transmission in your car."

Oh, the lessons we need to learn along the journey of life. Sometimes they're simple lessons about tollbooths, and sometimes they are more complicated character lessons that feel as though they take a toll on us. When home is a school, Mom and Dad are teachers of a variety of subjects in the classroom of life.

People Skills

Kids don't learn people skills by osmosis. They have to be taught appropriate manners and relationship skills. Teaching strategies vary depending upon the skill being taught. Sometimes modeling appropriate skills and simply talking about the importance of manners is enough. Most of the time, however, kids need direct instruction as well as many opportunities to role-play and practice their new skill. Let's look at some specific lessons we need to teach in our classroom.

Introductions

Try to be proactive in teaching kids how to handle being introduced to someone or introducing themselves to a person they do not know. The three most important keys to teach are:

1. Look them in the eye and smile.
2. Give them a firm handshake.
3. Respond with "It's nice to meet you."

If they have to introduce themselves to someone, the three keys still apply, but they have to be able to start the conversation themselves with "Hi! My name is Evan." The best way to teach children about introductions is to use role-play. One evening after dinner, tell your kids you want to teach them something they'll be able to use their entire life. If they are younger (age 4 through fifth or sixth grade), a simple lesson on how they are to respond when you introduce them to someone will do just fine. After talking about the three keys, let them practice with you and with each other. They'll probably laugh a lot, but the basic skill will have been taught, and you can build from there.

If your kids are junior high or high school age, they'll need to know how to handle both kinds of introductions: when someone

introduces them to another person and when they need to introduce themselves to someone (as in a job interview). You can use
the same strategies as you would with younger children, but don't
expect them to get excited about this. They'll roll their eyes a bit
and feel it is a silly exercise, but secretly they'll be glad you took the
time to teach them.

Phone Etiquette

The first step in phone etiquette is to create a system that works
for phone messages (scrap paper doesn't count). We have found
that a phone log by our main phone in the kitchen keeps messages
all in one place. I created our log on the computer, and there are
five columns on the log: Date/Time, Message For, Caller, Phone
Number, and Message organized on a three-ring binder. This provides a simple "fill in the blank" system that works even for new
message takers.

Children need to be instructed on how you want them to answer
the phone. At our home we've asked the kids to answer with "Hello,
this is the Savages'. Austin speaking." The first time I talked with
Austin about how to answer the phone, I "taught the lesson" as we
were driving. Austin was accompanying me on some errands, so I
took advantage of having a captive audience and taught him how
to answer the phone. Then we did some pretending with my cell
phone.

When we got home I showed him the phone log and did some
role-playing with taking a message. After his series of lessons, he
was ready to answer the phone. By the way, at our house you don't
answer the phone until you are nine years old. That's a rite of passage in the Savage family.

Thank-You Notes

Having a grateful heart and expressing thanks are two different
things. Kids need to be taught how to express written thanks when
they receive a gift or someone goes out of their way to do something for them. When they are just two or three years old, they

can sign their "name" on a card you have written. When my kids were preschoolers, I created a thank-you postcard on the computer using a font that looked like a child's writing. It looked something like this:

```
Dear _____.

Thank you for the _____.

I love it!

            Love,
```

As the kids grew older, they could write their own note with a little bit of help with spelling and spacing. Even throughout the preteen and teen years, the courtesy of sending thank-you notes, especially to grandparents and extended family, is very important.

Table Manners

The first lesson in table manners is learning how to set a table, which can be taught even to a preschooler. Fold the napkin in a rectangle or a triangle and place it to the left of the plate. Put the fork on the napkin and the knife and spoon to the right of the plate.

During the meal, there are basic lessons that can be taught:

1. Put your napkin on your lap.
2. Chew with your mouth closed.
3. Don't reach across someone. Ask for something to be passed.
4. Use the fork and spoon correctly (don't turn them upside down in your mouth).

Some parents like to teach table manners at a once-a-week or once-a-month candlelight meal. This provides a setting that is different from other meals and a great opportunity for a lesson. Others choose to simply teach the lessons at one of their family meals.

Being a Host or Hostess

When your child has a friend over, it's a great opportunity for the "how to be a good host" lesson. The best time to teach this lesson is right before their friend arrives. The basic elements of being a good host include:

1. Greet your friend at the door.
2. Defer to what your friend wants to do.
3. Serve your guest food and drinks before you serve yourself.
4. Walk your friend to the door and thank them for coming.

We recently took a friend of Austin's home after spending the night at our house. I pulled Austin aside before we got in the car and explained that when we arrived at Mason's house, it would be appropriate to walk Mason to the door to make sure he got inside and that one of his parents was home. I also shared with him that if he saw Mason's mom or dad, he needed to thank them for letting Mason come over. Austin responded with, "I have to do all of that?" I said, "Yes, if you want to be a good host and make people feel welcome and cared for. It's the right thing to do." He followed through when we arrived, and as he got back in the car he said, "Okay, that wasn't too bad."

Self-Management Skills

Our son Kolya has incredible self-management skills. Living in an orphanage for the first nine years of his life caused him to be very disciplined and self-reliant. If he hadn't taken care of himself and his things, no one else would have done it.

Self-management is something kids need to learn over the span of their childhood. A crash course in self-management, like Kolya had, is not the most effective classroom setting. Kids learn by what they see us do, by natural consequences (if I don't manage my time well, I don't get my homework done, and then I get a bad grade), and by direct instruction.

Self-management skills fall into two categories: personal appearance and personal discipline. Let's take a look at each of these.

Personal appearance skills consist of bathing or showering; washing, combing, and styling your hair; wearing deodorant (and remembering to put it on every day); and clothing care. During the preschool years, Mom and Dad have to help junior with personal care. Once he's in grade school, he needs to slowly take over the responsibility of his own care. Parents often have to be creative in teaching these skills, and the key is helping your child find ownership in the responsibilities. Here are some tips for teaching and training personal appearance skills:

Bathing/showering/washing hair. Allow your child to choose his own soap, shower gel, or scented shampoo. Give him ownership in selecting his personal care products. One mom found that her son suddenly began to take care of his hair regularly when he found an apple-scented shampoo that he thought was the coolest!

Deodorant. The most challenging part of wearing deodorant is helping your child to remember it every day. If you have a spare drawer in the bathroom, designate that drawer as your child's own. If you don't have a drawer, pick up a bathroom caddy similar to what college students use in a dorm. When all the products your child needs are in one place they call their own, it helps them to remember their routine.

Hair care. Make sure your child has his own comb or brush. For girls, make ponytails holders and barrettes easy to find. Include these items in their personal care drawer or caddy. Help your child to understand that choice comes with responsibility. If your daughter wants long hair, she has to care for it every day without an argument. If she can't carry the responsibility of caring for it, she'll need to have shorter hair until she is older.

Clothing care. For a child who has trouble matching clothes, you might store them in their closet or drawers as coordinated outfits.

At the Savage household, if I find clothes on the floor, they become mine for 30 days. We have explained to our kids that caring for your clothes is really about stewardship—taking care of the things God has given you. If you can't be responsible, then you lose the privilege of having very many choices in clothing.

Personal discipline skills refer to things like time management, study skills, doing your best work, and general organization. Before we go any further, however, it is important to understand that this is one of the last skills to develop over the span of an 18-year childhood. In researching our book *Got Teens?* Pam Farrel and I learned quite a bit about brain development. "The very last part of the brain to be pruned and shaped to its adult dimensions is the prefrontal cortex, home of the so-called executive functions—planning, setting priorities, organizing thoughts, suppressing impulses, weighing the consequences of one's actions. In other words, the final part of the brain to grow up is the part capable of deciding, I'll finish my homework and take out the garbage, and *then* I'll IM my friends about seeing a movie."[1]

It takes a great deal of patience for a parent to teach lessons and give assignments in the area of self-management. Let's look at some specific strategies for teaching other self-management skills.

Homework

What is your routine for homework? Kids respond well to routine. It helps them know their boundaries and manage their time. This year I made a "homework box" that contained crayons, colored pencils, and markers (just 10 to 12 of each). It also had pens, pencils, erasers, and a ruler. Each afternoon when the boys arrive home from school, our routine is the same: an after school snack in the kitchen and then a move to the dining room table for homework. The homework box made a big difference because it gave them easy access to the majority of the items they need to do their homework.

As kids enter junior high and high school, they may move to doing homework in their room, but they still need routine as well as your encouragement along the way. If their progress report indicates they are not turning in their work, they will need accountability as well. Most teachers will work with parents to communicate daily assignments in an effort to assist with accountability and teach kids self-management skills.

Time Management

Austin is a natural procrastinator, while Kolya often finishes his homework projects days, if not weeks, before they are due. Some of it has to do with temperament and some of it has to do with habit. Kids need to learn to manage their time by setting priorities and accurately estimating the amount of time a project will take.

A homework calendar can help in this process. When kids see the big picture and help determine a plan to complete the work, the project goes from an overwhelming task to manageable pieces. Daily homework can be put on the calendar too. My boys had their spelling test on Wednesday of each week. They got their new list each Thursday. We created a study routine that incorporated the same processes every day from Thursday through Wednesday to learn their words and prepare for the test.

Some children struggle with time management when it comes to getting ready for school in the morning. If you have one of those, all the nagging in the world will never teach them self-discipline. However, some creativity might help. Think of the tasks they need to accomplish on a typical school morning. Can you simplify them in any way for your child to remember? If your child responds to charts and stars, by all means use them to help develop routine.

At our home, we broke it down into something they can remember on one hand: The thumb is "bed" (make the bed), the pointer finger is "room" (they need to do a quick pick up in their room), the middle finger is "hair" (brush your hair), the fourth finger is "teeth" (brush your teeth), and the pinkie finger is "lunch" (make your lunch). There's nothing magical about it, and honestly I don't think there's an easy way to remember those steps, but by attaching them to each finger on their hand, they are able to remember them and manage themselves in the morning.

TIP: To teach a small child how to make their bed, have them sit on their pillow and pull the sheet right up to their belly. Then have them do the same with their blanket or comforter. Tell them to carefully crawl out of bed, trying not to move the covers (they can't do that completely, but it's fun to try!) and then straighten it a little more on each side of the bed. Voila! They successfully made their bed and can say, "I did that!"

Money Management

Managing money is a life skill we all need. When Mark and I married, it soon became evident that neither one of us understood good money management principles. We didn't understand the value of a budget. We made poor decisions regarding debt. We rarely used cash and didn't keep very good records. We gave to the church but didn't fully tithe. It was soon evident that we needed some remedial education. We had to "go to school" on money-managing principles.

You and I can save our children these kind of headaches by specifically teaching lessons of money management. There are many teaching moments in life when it comes to money. Let's look at a few.

TV commercials. Watch television for subtle messages about money, such as advertisements that say "No payment for 18 months." Begin your conversation by asking a question, such as, "Wow, no payment for 18 months. Do you think that is a good deal?" After some dialogue about what they might think, you can share with them, "Do you know that most people don't do anything to pay for their purchase during the 18 months? But that's not all. On most of those contracts, if they go even one day past the 18 months, they have to pay the interest that has compounded since their original day of purchase. And that's usually a very high interest rate and a lot of money added to what they now owe!" You might end your lesson there with, "It's a good thing to know those things so someday you don't get sucked in to an ad like that."

Grocery shopping. One of the best places to teach money matters is on a trip to the grocery store. Equip your kids with a calculator and show them how to figure out the price per pound or unit, asking them to help you figure out which brands give you the most for your money. You can also point out how many advertisements are designed to get you to buy more, such as "Two for $5." Unless the sign specifically says that one item is a certain price, most of the time when it says "Two for $5," the sign could also read "One for $2.50." They don't make signs like that, though, because they want you to buy two and spend more money.

Bill paying. Occasionally it is valuable to have your kids help with the bill paying. Have them add up all the bills to be paid and subtract it from the paycheck. They will at first be amazed at how large the paycheck is (they're not used to seeing money in the hundreds or thousands of dollars), but once they subtract all the bills they will also be amazed at how little is left over. This is a good exercise for kids grade school and older.

There are also many intentional lessons we can include in our lesson plan for money management. Here are a few.

The tithe lesson. God wants us to bring our best to Him. In the Bible He asks for our first fruits—the first ten percent of what we have. As parents we can begin teaching this at a young age. Mark and I gave our kids a $1 monthly allowance during their preschool years. We didn't give them a dollar, though. We gave them ten dimes. This helped them understand that for every dollar we have, God gets ten cents of it. As they grew older and began to get paid for odd jobs or even secured a job in their teen years, we continued to reinforce those early lessons about the beauty and value of tithing.

The saving lesson. In the same way that we need to give God ten percent, we also need to at least give ourselves ten percent. This is a life skill that our kids need to understand so they are prepared for learning to save as adults. When they were young, ten cents of their allowance went into a bank in their room. As they grew older, their ten percent of savings from their part-time job paycheck went directly into a savings account at the bank.

The pay cash/no debt lesson. It's tempting to let kids draw you into becoming their lender. "Mom, my paycheck doesn't come in until Friday. Can you give me money to go to the movies and I'll pay you back then?" It's tempting to say yes to a request like that, but it's not in their best interest. Can you imagine you or your spouse going to an employer and saying, "Can you spot me a loan until my paycheck comes in on Friday?" You would never do that. Instead, you have to manage your resources to last from one paycheck to the next, and our kids with jobs need to do the same. The general rule is: If you don't have the cash on hand, you can't do what you want to do.

The budget lesson. We all have some set expenses as well as unexpected expenses or entertainment opportunities. When a preteen or teenager begins to have some regular income coming in, whether its an occasional babysitting job or part-time employment at McDonald's, they need a plan to budget their money. This lesson happens when a parent sits down and asks the new earner some questions to help determine their budget: What do you need to pay for regularly? (For example, our teenagers who drive have to pay for a portion of their car insurance.) What things do you like to do with your friends that you need money for? What big events (homecoming dance, prom, mission trip, etc.) do you need to be saving toward? Once they answer those questions, they can determine how much to take out of every paycheck to plan toward having the money for their needs.

TIP: You can go to my website at www.jillsavage.org to find a sample of a budget notebook you can make with your kids. This includes paycheck worksheets they can modify to use each time they receive a paycheck. It also includes communication sheets and guidelines for parents to use in discussing money matters with their kids who have regular income coming in.

Home Management

A parent's job is to work themselves out of a job. It's a challenging predicament because everyone wants to be needed. If we work ourselves out of a job, we won't be needed anymore, right? No, that's not true at all. We're just needed in a different way as our children walk more and more toward independence.

It takes time to care for the place where we live, the responsibilities we have, and the things that we own. We have to manage the papers that come into the house (organizing), the clothes we wear (laundry), the space we live in (cleaning, mowing), the food we eat (meal preparation), and the things we need (shopping). When we accomplish these tasks, we are managing our home. Our kids need to know that it takes time and energy to care for the place we live in. They can learn those lessons by being involved and expected to participate in home management.

A child's first real effort at home management begins in the preschool years. This is when they bring home school papers or Sunday school papers. They also start collecting things, such as fast-food toys from kids' meals and other trinkets of all kinds. They also have toys they need to help manage. During the preschool and early elementary years, the parent will do most of the managing, but the parent needs to ask the child to help much of the time. This slowly introduces them to the concept that there are things in our life that need to be taken care of.

A preschooler can help with laundry by sorting clothes according to color. As they get into grade school they can not only sort, but also help fold the clothes. By junior high, you'll need to conduct some basic "how to do laundry" lessons to complete their education. From then on, they should be able to either assist with laundry responsibilities or completely be responsible for their own laundry. Do whatever works best for your family—but make the expectations clear as to how you expect each child to manage the laundry.

Saturday is "Home Management Day" at our house. We actually use that term to describe it. It's the day we all come together and take care of the house, the yard, and our own rooms. Most people work better with a list to follow. We have a standard home management to-do list that the family uses for Saturdays. The routine is the same each week:

- Strip bedsheets
- Make bed with fresh sheets
- Pick up, straighten, and organize your room
- Dust your room
- Vacuum your room
- Ask Mom what one thing she wants you to do in the house
- Ask Dad what he wants you to do in the yard

When you are finished with your list, you are free to spend the rest of your Saturday however you would like.

Preschoolers and early grade-schoolers will need help accomplishing their list. They don't have the focus or the physical ability to do those things listed above—but they still need to be involved. Yes, it's easier to do it on your own, but that is not what is best for them. They are our students and we are their teachers. They need to learn the lessons of home management because they will need to use them for life.

Make sure you don't skip over actually teaching them how to do each of their responsibilities. Oftentimes we expect things from our children that we've actually not taken the time to actually show them how to do. Here are some basic lessons.

Picking up/Organizing. First pick up all your clothes. If they are dirty, put them in the dirty clothes basket. If they are clean, fold them nicely or hang them up. Now begin to pick up anything on the floor and ask yourself, "Where is its home?" If it has a home, put it away. If it doesn't, you need to create a home for it or throw it away. Don't forget to pick up your closet and check under your bed.

Dusting. Start at your door and work around the room clockwise. Take everything off the shelf or piece of furniture you are dusting. Dust each item as you remove it and set it aside. Spray your dust

cloth with furniture polish (or you can buy the cloths that already
have the polish in them). Wipe the surface from one side to the
other. Place removed items back where they belong.

Vacuuming. Make sure everything is off the floor. Be careful to
never vacuum over the electrical cord of the vacuum—keep one
hand guiding the vacuum and the other guiding the cord. Vacuum
slowly from one side of the room to another.

By late elementary school, a child should be able to do their list
on their own with occasional coaching and assistance. I have my
fifth grade boys do it on their own three out of four weeks a month,
but once a month I work side by side with them to encourage them
and help them organize and de-junk. It's just nice to have someone
work with you occasionally. In fact, it says "I love you!" in a completely different way.

I do the same with my teenagers but usually less often than once
a month. Occasionally I try to make myself available to say, "Would
you like some help today?" It helps them get the job done faster, and
we often have great conversation we might not otherwise have.

Our kids also have their basics (the five-finger responsibilities)
and daily chores we call "family responsibilities." These are the tasks
that need to be done every day, such as emptying the dishwasher,
feeding the animals, collecting the trash throughout the house, and
running the vacuum on the main level high-traffic areas. The family
responsibilities are assigned by day with a chart on the refrigerator,
although our kids are now so accustomed to the schedule that they
rarely have to look at the chart.

What home management responsibilities are you doing that your
kids need to be doing? Where do you need to teach some lessons
that will equip them for life? What skills do they need to know in
order to someday live on their own? The answers to these questions
will be the foundation of your lesson plans as a parent.

Spiritual Disciplines

As a parent, our goal is to encourage our children to transition
from our faith and beliefs to making them their own faith and

beliefs. At some time they have to own it for themselves and find their own personal relationship with Jesus Christ. They too have to move from religion to relationship.

To help them do that, we can introduce them to the spiritual disciplines of attending church and youth group (being in community with other believers), reading their Bible, and praying.

I touched on much of that in the "Home as a Church" chapter earlier. However there are some lessons we can teach to help them develop some spiritual disciplines.

Bible reading. There are some great devotionals available for kids of all ages, starting with the preschool years and going right through the college years. Most devotionals help keep you in God's Word.

Praying. Teach your children to pray for more than their needs. We use the ACTS pattern for prayer with our kids. When they were young at bedtime, we'd have them fill in the blank:

> Adoration: God I praise You because You are _____ (holy, mighty, loving…).
>
> Confession: God, I'm sorry for _____.
>
> Thanksgiving: God, thank You for _____.
>
> Supplication: God, please help _____ (me, my friend, my sister…).

Now that they are older, they have an expanded way to talk with God. This is a great pattern for bedtime or a quiet time they might have. They can even write their prayers in a journal (just like writing a letter to God) as they get older.

Attending church and youth group. These lessons are the ones you teach with your life. If you occasionally don't go to church because you don't feel like it, your kids will learn that going to church isn't something valuable for your life; it's just an option you can do whenever it's convenient. If you walk away from a church service complaining about the length of the sermon or how bad the music was, they'll pick up that church is really about being entertained and sometimes the entertainment just isn't what it should be. Kids learn lessons about church from Mom and Dad. Make sure you aren't "teaching" incorrect lessons along the way.

Character and Values

It takes a lifetime of learning to become more Christlike, and even then we never will fully arrive. However, a life of character and integrity speaks volumes to the world around us. "Teaching kids to count is fine, but teaching them what counts is best," says actor Bob Talbert. As parents, we need to teach our kids that character counts. They need to know what character qualities are and how important they are in our relationships. Understanding character and integrity not only represents God well through our life, but also contributes to our interpersonal relationship skills.

There are dozens of character qualities found in the Bible and modeled in the way that Jesus Christ lived His life. Here is a list that is compiled from a series of booklets originally published by the Association of Christian Schools International:[2]

Character Quality	Definition	Scripture	Jesus' Example
Alertness	Knowing what is going on around me.	II Timothy 4:5a	Luke 8:43-48
Attentiveness	Listening with the ears, eyes, and heart	Proverbs 4:20-21	Mark 10:46-52
Carefulness	Taking one step at a time to do a job right	Ephesians 5:15	John 1:3
Contentment	Happy with what I have	I Timothy 6:6	Matthew 8:20
Courage	Meeting opposition with confidence	Joshua 1:7a	Matthew 27:34
Courtesy	Respectful words and ways with others	I Peter 3:8	John 18:29-38
Creativity	Doing something in a new way	Genesis 1:31a	John 9:1-7
Decisiveness	Able to make up my mind	Joshua 24:15	Matthew 21:12-13

Diligence	Working hard to accomplish a task	Proverbs 22:29	Matthew 26:36
Discernment	Able to see things as they really are	Hebrews 5:14	Luke 6:6-11
Eagerness	Being excited about doing a task	Jude 3b	John 3:1-21
Encouragement	Bringing hope and cheer to others	I Thessalonians 5:14	John 16:5-16
Fairness	Treating others equally	I Timothy 5:21b	John 20:24-29
Faith	Believing God will do what He says	Hebrews 11:1	Matthew 14:22
Flexibility	Willing to change my plans with a good spirit	Philippians 4:12	Mark 4:35-41
Forgiveness	Treating someone as though he never hurt me	Colossians 3:13	Luke 23:34
Friendliness	Eager to share myself with others	Proverbs 18:24	Luke 5:27-34
Generosity	Sharing what I have	II Corinthians 9:7	Matthew 14:15-21
Genuineness	Living the way your heart feels toward God	Joshua 24:14	Mark 14:32-42
Helpfulness	Ready to serve at any time	Isaiah 41:6	John 21:3-14
Honesty	Truthful words and ways	Ephesians 4:25	John 18:5
Honor	Deep respect for others	Hebrews 12:9	Luke 11:1-4
Hope	Quiet confidence in God's future for me	Psalm 62:5-6	John 14:1-6
Humility	Not taking credit for what God and others have done	Proverbs 16:19	John 13:5-17
Initiative	Making the first move without being asked	Proverbs 6:6-8	John 4:5-38
Joyfulness	Being happy inside and out	Psalm 35:9	Luke 18:15-17
Kindness	Tender and gentle words and ways	Ephesians 4:32	John 19:25-27

Love	Meeting another's need unselfishly	John 15:12	Mark 10:21
Loyalty	Supporting someone even when the going gets tough	Hebrews 3:14	Luke 4:1-12
Meekness	Patience without anger	Titus 3:2	Mark 14:53-65
Obedience	Doing what I am told with a happy, submissive spirit	Hebrews 13:17	Luke 2:40-52
Orderliness	Everything in its place	I Cor. 14:40	Mark 6:32-44
Patience	Walking with a happy spirit	James 5:8	John 21:15-22
Persistence	Doing a job when it gets tougher than expected	I Cor. 16:13	Luke 22:39-46
Promptness	Being on time	Ecclesiastes 3:1	John 11:1-44
Reliability	Being trustworthy at all times	Psalm 15:2, 4b	Luke 19:30-35
Resourcefulness	Applying special solutions to special problems	Proverbs 1:5	John 2:1-12
Responsibility	Doing what I know I ought to do	I Cor. 4:2	Matt. 17:24-27
Self-Confidence	Knowing God is working in and through me to do His will	Philippians 1:6	Luke 4:16-30
Self-Control	Doing something even when I don't feel like it	I Cor. 9:25a	Matt. 27:33-50
Tactfulness	Being able to do or say the right thing at the right time	Ecclesiastes 8:5	John 8:1-11
Tenderheartedness	Feeling the joys and hurts of others	Ephesians 4:32a	Luke 7:11-17
Thankfulness	Being grateful and saying so	I Thess. 5:18	Mark 14:3-9
Thoroughness	Completing a job	II Timothy 4:7	Luke 5:16-26

Thriftiness	Wise use of what I have	Luke 16:11	John 6:5-14
Tolerance	Accepting others even if they are different	James 2:1	Luke 10:38-42
Virtue	Doing what is right, in a Christlike way	II Peter 1:5a	Luke 4:16
Wisdom	Thinking God's way	Proverbs 4:7	Luke 20:19-25

When I first read through this list years ago, I knew this was something I needed to work on myself before I could teach lessons to my children about character. You might do as I did and go through and mark the qualities you know you need to understand better and be more known for. We'll never be perfect, but we can become more Christlike every day.

Our family has used this list in a variety of ways over the years. When I was homeschooling, we chose one character quality each month to study and work on. The definitions were especially helpful in understanding each quality. We no longer homeschool, but most summers we focus on one character quality a week or even one a day as an overview to understanding the importance of character.

When teaching character, choose a time to introduce the concept to your child—it could be during breakfast or driving to school or after dinner once a week. The conversation might go like this: "Austin and Kolya, our character quality this week is tenderheartedness. Tenderheartedness means that I feel the joys and hurts of others. We are tenderhearted when we are happy for someone when they are happy or when we are sad with someone when they are sad. Can you think of any situations where you have been or should have been tenderhearted?" We would then talk about some practical ways to apply this character trait. Then I would say, "Austin, could you please look up Ephesians 4:32 and read that verse to us? Kolya, would you look up Luke 7:11-17 and read those verses so we can see how Jesus modeled tenderheartedness for us?" We'd take a few minutes to read the verses and talk about them. I'd close our lesson out with, "Let's watch for ways we can be tenderhearted this week." That's it—less than ten minutes of time for some foundational

information to be given. From then on we would have continued
discussion about it, and I would look for ways to either affirm them
when they were tenderhearted or show them situations where they
could choose tenderheartedness.

Lesson Plans

When home is a school, Mom and Dad need to be proactive as
they consider the lessons they need to teach. Each child is unique
and has a different way of learning. If you can modify lessons for
each child, dependent on their learning style, it will be an even more
effective way to teach.

In the same way that a teacher ponders what to teach and how to
teach it, we have to do the same with people skills, self-management
skills, home-management skills, spiritual disciplines, and character
traits. And in the same way that a teacher lays out lesson plans, we
also need lesson plans to help us strategize when and how we will
educate our children in our home that is also a school.

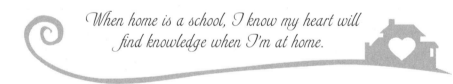

*When home is a school, I know my heart will
find knowledge when I'm at home.*

8

Home as a Museum

*Enjoy the little things, for one day you may look back
and realize they were the big things.*

ROBERT BRAULT

Whave a response. "I want to go to the new
Abraham Lincoln Presidential Museum in Springfield, Illinois. And
I want you and I to go by ourselves!" I love history, and my idea of
going to a museum includes reading every word at every exhibit.
I don't want to miss any part of history that I can learn, but my
children don't enjoy museums to that extent. My husband doesn't
love museums either, but he loves me! The two of us took a trip to
Springfield and spent the day at the museum, and it was one of the
best birthday presents ever.

A history museum displays artifacts from the past. It completes
a picture for us concerning where we've come from and paints a
picture we might not otherwise be able to see. When home is a
museum, it serves as a place to remember the past in our lives and
in lives that were lived before us. It also serves as a memorial to the
work that God has done in our life.

Our God Stories

It's nothing but an old Coke bottle box that we found at an auc-
tion. Hanging on our family room wall, it houses a display in our

family's museum. Each item in the display has a "God story" that
goes along with it.

There's a small piece of fabric cut from some vertical blinds we
once had. Those brand-new expensive blinds were given to us at a
time when Mark was unemployed. It is a reminder that God not
only provides for our daily needs, but occasionally our frivolous
wants as well.

There's a communion cup sitting on one shelf. When we planted
a new church seven years ago, a well-established church heard about
our new church and gave us a communion set they weren't using
anymore. We had been praying that God would provide a communion set because we didn't have the money to buy one.

There's a miniature VW Bug "Herbie" car. It's a reminder of a
time when we didn't have very much money to buy a second vehicle,
but God matched us up with someone who had a car that didn't
cost very much money. I drove that car back and forth to Butler
University as I finished my music education degree.

Next to the shadow box is a photo collage commemorating our
adoption journey. I took a frame made for eight photos and put a
mix of pictures, letterhead, Scripture, and even a copy of a check
we received that tells the story of a $36,000 adoption that God
provided every penny for in just nine months! (If you want to read
the whole story, you can find it on my website at www.jillsavage.
org.) This collage, as well as every item in the Coke bottle box, tells
the God stories of our family.

In the Bible, after Israel crossed the Jordan River into the Prom-
ised Land, God gave Joshua the following instructions: "Choose
twelve men…and tell them to take up twelve stones from the
middle of the Jordan…and put them down at the place where you
stay tonight…In the future, when your children ask you, 'What do
these stones mean?' tell them…" (Joshua 4:2-3,6-7). Those stones
were to be a reminder of a mighty act of God, and God wanted
those stories to be shared with generations yet to come.

God moves in our lives all the time. Sometimes we miss His
hand at work because we're not looking for it. Sometimes life is

moving along at such a pace that everything seems like a blur and we don't have time to see Him work. And sometimes we simply forget to give Him the credit.

When home is a museum, credit is given where credit is due. The memorials displayed are a tribute to God's work in the family. What God stories does your family have? What could you display to represent them? How could you follow Joshua 4:6, "In the future, when your children ask you, 'What do these stones mean?' tell them…"

My boys love the Herbie car in our display. When they ask if they can play with it, I gladly pull it down. But I tell them that I first have to share with them the story of the Herbie car. (They have heard the story so many times they can tell their friends when they come over.) I want them to know, remember, and experience a part of their rich heritage of faith.

Tell the Family Stories

As a young child I can remember going to several family cemeteries with my father and grandfather. They took the time to tell us the stories of the family members who were buried there—some who had fought in the Civil War as well as WWI and WWII. They shared the stories that had been passed on to them by my great-grandfather. Now it was time to pass on the stories to my children. I chose Memorial Day as the perfect time for our trip.

It had been many years since I'd been to those cemeteries, and my children had never had the opportunity to hear all the stories I had heard throughout my childhood. I asked my parents to join us, and we launched on a full-day tour of cemeteries in Southern Indiana. I could have never found several of the burial sites by myself, as many are tucked away in places where there isn't even road access to them anymore. Some were in pristine shape set next to a little white church, while others required us to wade through creeks and walk through waist-high grass.

Each stop unfolded a new piece of family history. We visited the graves of family members who traveled by wagon train, men who had fought in the Civil War, and babies who had died at birth. We even heard one story about a relative who had deserted during the Civil War and hid in a covered wagon to avoid being caught. We heard it all—the good and the bad. Each story was like a piece of a puzzle, and by the end of the day, we were able to put all the pieces together and see a clearer picture of our rich family heritage.

It was a powerful experience for the kids, one they will not soon forget. It deepened their sense of family identity, widened their understanding of who came before them, and heightened their sense of awareness of the stories and legacy they will someday leave behind as well.

When home is a museum, it is also a tribute to the family who came before us. If you have the ability to tell family stories with or without a cemetery tour, I encourage you to take the time to do it. Here are some tips for making such an effort successful:

- Take notes. Our oldest daughter, Anne, served as the secretary on our trip. She wrote down the directions to each cemetery as well as the stories that went with each grave site.

- Use a video camera. This allows you to record the stories as they are being told.

- Take pictures of the gravestones. This gives you the possibility of putting together a scrapbook of the pictures and the stories.

- Take crayons and paper. Even younger children can learn how to do gravestone rubbings to read the words on a worn gravestone.

- Ask questions. You might start with, "Grandma, what do you remember about your childhood?" or "Dad, tell me what you remember about Uncle Joe."

Don't miss the opportunity to hear and record the stories of yesteryear. You might begin by talking about family members who died fighting for our country, using the Fourth of July or Memorial Day as a springboard. Once the door is open for storytelling, walk through it completely to capture the history and heritage of your family.

Use Creativity

After our cemetery tour, Anne dug through boxes and boxes of pictures to find fragile, yellowing pictures of the people we heard stories about. Over a period of several months she created a scrapbook of the tour we had experienced as a family. The stories that had been passed down verbally were now recorded in writing. That book, given as a Christmas gift to her grandmother and granddad, will now become a family heirloom that is passed from one generation to the next. It's a marker, a memorial to help us remember.

If scrapbooking isn't your thing, maybe a little bit of technology might excite you. A video or DVD movie of family members telling their stories would be an incredible way to preserve history. You can interview family members about their growing up years and the stories they remember hearing about their relatives.

Maybe you have Grandma's old recipe box. You can type up the recipes she used most frequently and make a family cookbook. By including copies of her original recipe cards on some of the pages, family members can see her handwriting and benefit from her time-tested family recipes that have been passed down through the years. A short biography would help introduce future family members to Grandma and her home cooking.

Journals and diaries can prove to be wonderful museum pieces for the family. If you have any of these from generations past, you can display them on a bookshelf as a visual reminder of your heritage.

Start Now

Someday you and I will be a part of somebody's past. Our words, pictures, and stories will be passed on to generations to come. What are you doing to keep your family museum alive?

One mom I know kept a journal circulating between herself and her two sisters. Rather than writing them each individual letters, this mom started a journal that read like a letter. She would journal over the span of a week and then mail it to one of her sisters. That sister would journal for a week and then pass it on to the final sister. Once she read and wrote her entries, she mailed it back to start the circuit again. Not only does this simplify the communication process, but it provides a beautiful set of stories to pass on to their children someday.

Maybe you could scrapbook the stories of your family. Or maybe a shadow box could be hung on your wall to hold items that represent the God stories or the family stories.

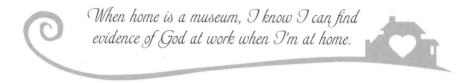

When home is a museum, I know I can find evidence of God at work when I'm at home.

PART III
The Details

9

Home as a Playground

Fill your home with love and laughter.

THOMAS KINKADE

I love to people-watch. I find it fascinating to sit back and watch the world move around me. I especially love to sit at a playground and watch children hard at play. Some are playing tag; others are digging in the sandbox. One child climbs up the stairs to slide, and another is content to swing for what seems like hours. Regardless of what activity they choose to participate in at the playground, there is one thing for sure—they are all having fun.

Families are meant to have fun together. A playful spirit and a good measure of laughter are medicine for the soul. When home is a playground, there's an intentional effort to have fun and play together as a family.

Laughter Is Good Medicine

From my personal observation, the average child laughs hundreds of times per day. The average adult laughs less than a dozen times each day. When did we become so uptight?

Not only is laughter good for the soul, it's great for the body. "Laughter can lower blood pressure, increase muscle flexion, and trigger a flood of endorphins—the brain chemicals that can bring on euphoria. Laughter profoundly affects our immune systems. Gamma interferon, a disease-fighting protein, rises with laughter. So do B cells, which orchestrate our body's immune response. Laughter can also shut off the flow of stress hormones—the fight-or-flight compounds that come into play when we feel hostility, rage, and stress."[1]

My favorite television show is *America's Funniest Home Videos (AFV)*. My family loves the show too, but they get even more of a kick out of watching me laugh all the way through it. I laugh and laugh and laugh. On Sunday nights we often watch *AFV* and *Extreme Makeover: Home Edition*. We all love the shows and we laugh until our stomach hurts watching *AFV,* and then we pass the Kleenex box around watching the encouraging but often emotional *Extreme Makeover: Home Edition*. It's good to laugh and cry together.

Make Play a Priority

My friend Lora has a welcoming home. She's also set up her home intentionally for play. Right in the middle of their living area she has a bistro table and two chairs. An ongoing game of chess is always set up on the table. One day when I was visiting her, her boys tumbled in from school. After a quick snack, they immediately sat down and played about 15 minutes of chess. It was ready and available, so it made for a logical choice.

Ever since that day I've been watching for a bistro set at a garage sale. I'd like to do the same; however, I'd like to do it with puzzles. We like to do puzzles together as a family, so I'd have a puzzle going at all times. I'd like something classier than a card table out all the time, but I don't have the money for a new bistro set. I'll just keep looking and someday I'll find it.

Is play easy to do at your house? In every one of our homes, my husband and I have strived to have some section of the house serve as a toy room. This is the kids' room—a place where we keep dress up clothes, buckets of Legos, a pretend kitchen, and a variety of miscellaneous toys. On the bookshelf in the toy room I also keep craft and activity books as well as crayons, markers, craft supplies (wiggle eyes, pipecleaners, glue sticks, foam shapes, child-safe scissors, etc.), and construction paper. It's set up to encourage imagination, creativity, and lots of fun.

Games, Games, and More Games

Games not only build community in a family, they are also valuable in a child's development. They facilitate the development of strategic thinking, hand/eye coordination, and quick decision making. In addition, they require concentration as well as focused attention.

Writing for www.scholastic.com, child psychologist Alvin Rosenfeld states that traditional board games aid the development of important social skills in children, including cooperation, self-control, confidence, independent thinking and decision making, curiosity, empathy, communication, teamwork, vocabulary development, and patience. For younger children, game playing helps them learn to participate in group activities, handle disappointments, understand rules and structure, and learn to play fairly. And game players of all ages have to learn to win and lose graciously.

However, the most valuable benefit of playing games is the human interaction they require. Bottom line—we have to talk to one another. Conversations while playing a board game range from encouragement to teasing to what happened on the playground yesterday at school. That's precious conversation for a parent to have with a child.

Most kids love to play board games. I'm sure one of the reasons why they enjoy playing games with Mom and Dad is because they have Mom and Dad's full attention. It's rather difficult to play Uno or Hi Ho! Cherry-O while doing something else. However, if your family hasn't had the habit of playing games together, it may take some urging on your part. Too many children today are accustomed to playing fast-paced video games that do not require interaction with other people. In other words, they are self-focused activities that keep kids isolated rather than interacting with others. If that is what they are accustomed to, it may take some convincing to begin game playing as a family. But don't give up or cave in to their whining. Let them know you're doing something new and everyone will participate. They'll soften over time as they come to realize how much fun it can be (although they probably won't admit it).

Know your games and select according to the time you have. You'll rarely see the Game of Life or Monopoly taking less than an hour to play, but a game of Uno can be played in less than ten minutes. Sometimes you have to choose your games based on the amount of patience you have as a parent. There are just some days that I don't have the brainpower for Monopoly. That's when I need a no-brainer game like Uno.

The next time you sit in a doctor's office with your child, try playing a game like Riddly Riddly Ree rather than attempting to read a magazine. You simply select something in the room and the other person has to guess what it is. We play it by saying:

"Riddly Riddly Ree. I see something you don't see and the color is blue." Then the other person begins looking for blue things in the room and guessing which one it might be. Kids love it up through late grade school.

On vacations or holiday breaks you might try playing an ongoing game all week. When we go to my parents' condo in Florida for summer vacation, we usually have a 1000-piece puzzle on the coffee table and an Uno tournament going all week. Instead of playing to win each game, we're playing for points. The person with the most points at the end of the week is the winner.

When we were in the process of adopting our son Kolya at the age of nine from an orphanage in Russia, we found playing games together crossed the language barrier. We had to make two trips to Russia—the first trip to meet Kolya and confirm we wanted to adopt him, and the second trip to go to court, finalize the adoption, and bring him home.

As I was packing for the trip, a friend mentioned that I might want to pack some games. Since he was nine, he was certainly old enough to play games. I packed Uno, Trouble, and Memory. On our first trip we played so many games of Memory I was seeing it in my sleep, but Kolya loved the game. The first time we showed it to him we didn't even need a translator to explain to him the concept. We showed him a couple of sample plays and he caught right on. The same with the game of Trouble—he caught on so quickly that before long we were teaching him the colors in English and he was teaching us the colors in Russian. We did the same with the numbers.

After we came home with this new member of our family who knew no English, games helped us cross the language barrier as a family. Each night we played and laughed together to begin the bonding process. Kolya was fully speaking English within three months, and the games played a big role in that process.

When home is a playground, trust grows, bonds are strengthened, and relationships deepen. But games aren't the only option for fun.

Family Recreation

Last summer we began a tradition of a Sunday afternoon family baseball game in the yard. It not only gave us exercise but was fun for everyone. If you have a basketball hoop, try a family game of H-O-R-S-E, where if you miss the basket doing the assigned shot you earn a letter in the word "horse." If you have less time, then try P-I-G.

A picnic in the park is always fun. Not only does it get you out of the house and away from the phone, laundry, and other things that keep screaming for your attention, it allows for focused attention on every member of the family. How about roller-skating, miniature golf, bowling, or ice-skating? A day trip to a nearby state park would give you the opportunity to hike, fish, or swim at a beach.

Playing together in the kitchen is fun too. When the kids were small I would make cookie dough while they were napping. After they woke up we'd work together to shape the cookies, bake them, and eat them right out of the oven. When it came to cutout Christmas cookies, I learned it was much easier to make the dough, cut out the cookies, bake them myself, and then let the kids help decorate the prepared cookies with colored icing and sprinkles. Now that my kids are older, they help with the process from beginning to end. It's not only fun to bake together, but also a great place to teach about food safety, measurements, and fractions.

Family recreation can have an added dimension if Mom and

Dad have a playful spirit. Pam and her husband, Gary, used to enjoy hot summer days with their two boys and a little water play. They would fill up two five-gallon buckets with water and arm each family member with a Cool Whip bowl. An all-out water fight ensued. There was no expense, just a lot of laughter and fun.

If you are looking for fresh ideas for family fun, check out more ideas at www.familyfun.com.

Fun in the Car

When traveling with kids, road trips can either be a recipe for disaster or an opportunity for fun. Whether it's a three-hour trip to Grandma's or a cross-country sightseeing vacation, the success of the road trip will be determined by the attitude and preparedness of the parents.

When my kids were small, I never traveled anywhere without a bottle of bubbles. By holding the bubble wand up to the air conditioner or heater vent, I could fill the car with bubbles in less then a minute. This would help distract a crying toddler or entertain a preschooler for the last ten minutes of running errands. When stuck in a traffic jam, you can invite others into your fun by opening your car windows and letting the bubbles pour out of your car. Sometimes it's nice to spread a little bit of fun to the world around you.

Car trips usually mean special snacks for our family. The only time I buy "cheese in a can" to spray on crackers is when we make a long car trip. Saving some food purchases for special occasions only can make events like long car trips an opportunity for a rare treat. I also make a trip to the dollar store when preparing for "fun on the road." My dollar store purchases provide a special treat for every hour we're in the car. Sometimes it's something to eat, but most of the time it's something to keep the kids busy: a notebook with a fancy pen, a crossword puzzle book, a coloring book and crayons, a package of pipe cleaners to create with—anything that provides a new opportunity for fun in the car.

Give Ownership

If you want your kids' full participation in the fun you have as a family, give them ownership in determining some of the activities. At the beginning of every summer I sit down with my kids and we make up two lists. One list is fun things we can do at home and the other is fun things we can do away from home. When I hear "I'm bored!" I pull out one of the lists for them to remember all the options they have to do.

As kids grow older, it's important that they become part of the decision making for family recreation. This gives them a vested interest in the activity and helps them feel they were a part of the planning. If you have a regular family night, you might try alternating the leadership of your evenings among the different members of your family. This works well with older grade-schoolers and teenagers.

Kids long to belong. Belonging happens when you are a contributing member of a group. Our kids want to do more than be told what they are going to do—they want to help make decisions about what we're going to do as a family. This is not only valuable in maturing their decision-making processes, but is also valuable in helping them feel they are an important member of the team known as family.

A Playful Heart

I have often said that a mom's ability to have fun is directly proportioned to her ability to stand a mess. Moms who don't mind a mess find it easier to have fun than moms who like things neat and clean all the time. I believe that really is true and is helpful for us to understand.

I also think that age robs us of a sense of playfulness. Children increase our responsibilities, and as responsibilities increase we grow more serious and less playful. Our personalities and temperaments also contribute to our fun quotient. With this in mind, when home is a playground, it isn't just for the benefit of the children; it's for our benefit as well. We need the laughter, the lightheartedness, and the distractions from the daily responsibilities of life.

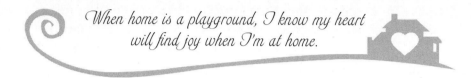

When home is a playground, I know my heart will find joy when I'm at home.

10

Home as a Business Office

Be warm. Be welcome. Be home.

ANNIE DANIELSON

In just one afternoon I found $170 for our family plus an additional $20 each month. Was it from the efforts of working a part-time job? Cutting coupons? Canceling the cable television? Nope. It was actually easier than any of those strategies. I found that money simply by running an efficient home office.

Every home is a mini business office. Bills have to be paid, insurance papers filed, warranties tracked, and banking transactions made. There are numbers to keep, dates to be noted, and money to manage. We've got to manage multiple schedules, doctor and dental appointments, transportation, and responsibilities for the upkeep of a home.

When it's just the two of you, it's possible to keep tabs on these things with a little bit of time each week. But the more family members you add to your home, the more time it takes to manage the "business" of the family.

Where Did I Put That?

Organization is key to running the family's business. I was first introduced to the need for good office organization when I received our oldest daughter's Social Security card in the mail…when she was one month old. What was I to do with a card she wouldn't need for another 20 years? Where should I keep the card? Should I note the number anywhere else? What would we need it for? Filing taxes? Opening bank accounts? This was just the beginning of managing the paperwork of what would someday be a good-sized family.

A good filing system is a must for running an efficient business office. If you don't have a filing system in place, make a goal to get yourself organized in the next few weeks. An organized system can be created on just about any budget.

Start with a two- or four-drawer file cabinet. If the cabinet is not set up for hanging files, you can purchase hanging file frames for the drawers. If you are working with a limited budget, look for a used file cabinet at garage or estate sales or skip the whole file cabinet thing and go for plastic crates that many college students use in dorm rooms. Most plastic crates are designed to accommodate hanging files and are available in a variety of sizes and colors.

A frugal way to file is to use the more expensive hanging files for filing categories and less expensive manila or colored index folders within the hanging files. For instance, I have a hanging file titled "Personal Papers." Within that file there are seven manila folders, one for each member of my family. Inside those folders you will find each person's Social Security card, passport (if they have one), birth certificate, high school transcripts, etc. (Some people may choose to keep some of these documents in safety deposit boxes at the bank or fireproof security boxes kept at home.)

I like to think of filing in two ways: short-term and long-term. Short-term files are for documents and paperwork that come into the house, need to be kept for a few days, weeks, or months, and then discarded. Long-term files are for paperwork that needs to be kept six months or more.

We have an extra bedroom in our home that we use for an office, and that's where we have a four-drawer file cabinet that holds our long-term files. (Before we had an extra bedroom, we had a corner of our dining room set aside for a makeshift office.)

Our short-term files are kept right in the midst of where our family lives, where we open our mail, and where we're likely to see it every day—in the kitchen. I use a crate to create a file drawer right on the kitchen counter. My sister Juli uses a three-ring binder with a folder for each person. The kind of system doesn't matter, just create a system that works for you. This helps keep the counter clutter at bay.

Short-Term Files

Start by organizing your short-term papers. What kinds of papers do you tend to misplace? Make a folder for them. What papers are currently in piles on your counter? Sort them into piles, assign a category to them, put the category name on a file folder, and place the papers into the file.

What are some examples of short-term files? Here are some ideas to get the wheels turning.

Bills to Pay

Each time I bring in the mail, it's either junk mail or bills to be paid. Regardless of whether you pay the bills or your spouse handles that duty, you need a place to put the statement you just received. If you already have a place that's working for bills, keep doing what works. If your tendency is to leave them on the kitchen counter because you really don't have a designated place for them to live until you pay them, then it's time to establish a "Bills to Pay" file.

Current Medical Receipts

Medical receipts and insurance papers need to be carefully managed each month. This file can be a holding place for both doctor receipts and "Explanation of Benefits" (EOB) documents. Once a month these documents can be matched up, evaluated for accuracy, and then refiled in a long-term file for taxes. Insurance companies can make mistakes—make sure you check your benefits each time a claim is filed.

Taxes

Every January we start getting tax documents such as W2s,

annual giving receipts from church and other nonprofits, and interest reports from the bank. These and other documents collected throughout the year are needed when filing taxes. Keeping a short-term "Taxes" file helps keep these documents in one place until it's time to file your taxes.

Family Member Files

It can be very helpful for every family member to have his or her own short-term file. This is where miscellaneous papers such as project outlines for homework, mail that needs to be kept for a period of time, or the instruction sheet your son printed out for his favorite online game that got left on the floor in the family room can be stored. When you find these homeless items, you can simply tuck them in the appropriate file. When they ask, "Mom, have you seen my paper about...?" simply suggest they check their file. These short-term files are sorted every month.

Invitations

Invitations to birthday parties, weddings, and graduation parties are usually a welcome sight when sorting through a stack of bills and junk mail. After opening the invitation, noting it on the calendar, and calling in an RSVP, the invitation can be discarded. But what if it contains important information, such as gift registration or driving directions? An invitation file gives you a short-term place to put the invitation so when it's time to go to the celebration, you know right where to find the information.

Store Promotions

I keep coupons in my purse, but sometimes store promotions are too big to lug around but still valuable to keep. Maybe your favorite catalog company is offering free shipping during the month of December with the use of a special code on your order form. When you receive this offer in the mail, tuck it in your "Store Promotions" file to be retrieved when you are ready to place your order.

Current Project Files

Short-term projects often have some paperwork involved, so make a file folder to help keep the information together. It might be handy to have a "Family Vacation" file to keep reservation documents, tourism brochures, and other information collected during the planning stage. If you have a family member preparing for a mission trip, a "Mission Trip" file keeps correspondence and information about the trip in one place. If you are remodeling a room in the house and have paint samples, pictures from a magazine, or contractor contact information, you can create a "Remodeling" folder to keep all the information together.

TIP: Always keep a few extra empty file folders in your notebook, crate, or file cabinet drawer. This will help keep you organized because it makes creating a new file very easy.

Once your short-term files are organized, you'll need to manage them. Don't be overwhelmed—it's just a matter of developing some new habits. Every day when the mail comes in, use your file system. When you go through the kids' backpacks after school, use the files. Once a month, take 15 minutes to go through and discard anything that is no longer needed.

Long-Term Files

Once your short-term files are established, it's time to set up your long-term files. These files will help you keep documents organized for tax purposes, good record keeping, or simply being able to put your hands on any document you need at a moment's notice.

Here are some questions for you to answer to help determine what long-term files you need:

- What do you do with bill statements after they've been paid?
- Where do you put receipts so you can find them if an item needs to be returned?
- Where do you put warranty documents?

- Where do you put instruction books for your electronic or household items?

If you answered "I don't know" to any of those statements, you probably need to create a long-term file for those documents. Here are some long-term files to consider.

A to Z Receipt Files

Filing shopping receipts in 26 alphabetical files will greatly reduce your time searching for a receipt when it's needed. If you shop at one store frequently, you might make one file for that specific store. In our file drawer we have our 26 alphabetical folders plus a folder for Wal-Mart—because it feels as though I live at Wal-Mart some weeks.

Medical Documents

Once a doctor receipt has been matched up with insurance paperwork, these documents can be put in a long-term "Medical" file. These may be needed for taxes and would be needed if you were ever audited. They might also be needed if you ever need to change doctors and/or insurance programs.

Utility/Credit Card Statements

Once a bill is paid, it is wise to keep your statements for up to 12 months. This allows you to review and compare your bills to make sure you are being charged correctly.

Warranty and Instruction Files

"Warranty" and "Instruction" files can be kept alphabetically or by category (appliances, computer, electronics, etc). Attach the receipt to the warranty information in case you need to return an item that is under warranty. Keep warranties until they expire.

Home and Auto Titles and Insurance

Titles are needed to transfer ownership when you sell a car or home. Insurance information is needed when a claim is filed. Keep these in a safe, well-labeled location.

TIP: Every January, it's a good idea to have a "File Cleaning" day to either discard some of your long-term files if they are no longer needed or move them into their "Seven-Year Storage." Most tax consultants advise keeping tax documents for seven years from their filing date. At the end of each year you can move what is in each of your files into a 9x12 manila envelope for its seven-year storage. Mark the envelope with clear identification and put it in whatever seven-year file system you use (boxes in the basement or attic, an extra drawer in a file cabinet, etc.).

Other Organization Strategies

Clothing

There is great frugality in passing on gently used clothing from one child to the next. To do this effectively, it takes an organizational system that works well for you. Investing in some large plastic containers is usually a great place to start. After filling a container with clothing that one child has outgrown and the next child is not yet wearing, document the clothing in the storage container on a 4x6 index card attached to the outside of the box. Rather than listing every item in the box, use general descriptions to describe the contents:

Boys underwear sizes 4—5

Boys jeans sizes 4 and 5

Boys winter coat size 6x

Several pair boys socks size 11—4

Keepsakes

Every person in the family has special items, school papers, newspaper clippings, and other memorabilia they want to keep. Having a place to put these items is important for keeping clutter under control. Once again a large plastic storage box can work well. One box for each person in the family can be stored in their bedroom or closet. Identify the box with something like "Erica's Keepsakes" on the outside. When a child wants to keep something special, you can ask them to take it to their room and put it in their keepsakes box.

TIP: Kids like to keep everything. You will need to teach them how to be the manager of their school papers. From their first year of school, help them learn to keep meaningful work and discard the ordinary, everyday stuff. For special trinkets and other items that aren't really keepsakes but still need a place to be kept, have each child keep a smaller box in their room marked something like "Erica's Treasure Box." This is where they can keep the special toy they got at McDonald's or the note from a friend they don't want to throw away yet. Once a month, ask them to go through their treasure box and make sure they really need everything that's in there. When the box if full, tell them they have to get rid of some things in the box if they want to keep new treasures.

Toys

Make it routine to conduct regular purging sessions. There are times it is valuable to do this task without children, but there is also value in teaching children how to declutter and make wise choices. If your kids insist on keeping items you would like to get rid of, put them in storage containers and move them to the garage or attic. If the kids ask for them, give the items back. If they never mention them again, discard them or give them away after four to six months.

Backpacks

Backpacks can often get dumped right inside the door unless

you designate a place for them. As soon as your kids get home from school, have them empty their backpacks and lunch boxes and place their book bags in their "home." As soon as homework is finished, have them repack their bags so they are ready for the next morning. It is helpful if the home for the backpacks is near the door so it's easy access when they come home from school and when they leave in the morning. Some heavy-duty hooks on a wall near the door or large cubby hole shelving would do the trick just fine. One mom found some old school lockers and placed them right in her breezeway. Each child had their own locker for their book bag, coat, and other things they needed to take to school.

Schedule Management

Sometimes it feels as though I'm more of an air traffic controller than a mom. That's because I have to manage the appointments and transportation needs for seven people! When home is a well-run business office, schedules need to be strategically managed.

Start with a central calendar. It could be posted on the refrigerator, hanging on a wall, or it could be a desk calendar that is kept by the phone. Use whatever style and location works best for you. The central calendar is the one everyone uses for communication.

My husband keeps his own personal calendar, but evening and weekend appointments are transferred to the family calendar. This helps me know when he has a 6:00 PM meeting, which requires me to plan for dinner at 5:00 that evening. The kids have the responsibility of either putting their practice schedules, musical rehearsals, and school programs on the calendar themselves or getting me the information so I can put it on the calendar.

I had always used a planner for my personal calendar needs. However, this past year I decided to go to an electronic calendar with an upgrade to a PDA phone. My phone synchronizes with Microsoft Outlook on our computer, so I can carry my calendar everywhere I go. I still display a paper calendar in the kitchen, but it is simply printed out from the computer every month.

I can't believe how much easier the PDA has made my life. The other day I entered 22 ball games on our family calendar in just a matter of minutes. I always have my calendar with me for scheduling dental appointments six months down the road. And I have a built-in reminder for birthdays, anniversaries, and other important dates.

Each spring I try to be proactive with our schedules by going to the school's website and getting the next school year calendar entered into our calendar. Knowing the dates my children will be out of school almost a year in advance helps in scheduling doctor and dental appointments or a long weekend trip to Grandma's.

When Joey needs to be at the dentist's office, Susie has piano lessons, and Jason's baseball practice all occur at the same time, that's when home becomes like an air traffic control center! A well-kept calendar helps with transportation needs too. If all the dates are entered onto the family calendar, you can more easily thwart a collision of important appointments. Good organization also helps you group your transportation needs to best use time and fuel in getting everyone where they need to be. That's another way that running a good business office saves on financial resources.

Manage Your Business

If we take the time to manage the business of our home well, our efforts will pay emotional and financial dividends in the end. When I'm prepared and my time is well thought out, I'm less stressed. When the kids' "hand-me-down" clothes are organized, I save money by knowing where the next-size tennis shoes are.

Remember the $170 I found at the beginning of the chapter? I "earned" it from our wireless phone company, who had us on a different pricing plan than what we had signed up for. When I looked carefully at the bill and called customer service, they admitted the mistake and credited the incorrect charges from the time the mistake was made several months earlier. The credits totaled $170. The additional $20 a month came from an advertisement in the mail for our DSL Internet service. We were paying $35 a month for the same service the company was now offering for $15 a month. They didn't offer the new price to their old customers, but when I called and asked about it, they said, "Sure, you can get on that plan." It appears some people are paying $35 a month and others are paying $15 a month for exactly the same thing. I would still be paying $35 a month if I hadn't taken the time to manage the business in my home.

My job as a mother at home saves us money and stress simply by my ability to give attention to detail in managing the business of our home. Even if your husband is the primary "business manager" in your home, it is still valuable for you to understand and use any organizational system set up in your home. Your home is a business office, and you are a valuable manager or assistant manager of that business.

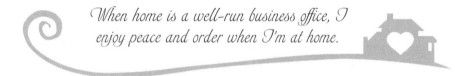

When home is a well-run business office, I enjoy peace and order when I'm at home.

11

Home as a Hospitality House

Charity should begin at home, but should not stay there.

PHILLIP BROOKS

We had just sat down at the dinner table when one of our younger boys asked where their 19-year-old brother, Evan, was. I started to answer the question, but when I heard the garage door slam shut, I responded, "Well, he was at the pool, but it looks like he's home now." I walked into the kitchen to greet Evan, only to find Evan's friend Collin. "Collin, what are you doing here?" I asked. "Hi, Mrs. Savage. I'm looking for Evan. Is he here?" I responded that Evan was at the pool, to which Collin replied, "Oh, could I borrow a swimsuit?" "Sure, Collin." I said, "Just run up to Evan's bedroom and see what you can find."

We all laughed about how we thought Collin was Evan just a few minutes earlier. But then Erica captured the essence of our thoughts when she said, "You know, it's neat that our friends feel welcome enough to just walk in and mesh right into the family."

When home is a hospitality house, it's a place that feels safe and welcoming to anyone who enters its doors. Whether kids are hanging out at your house or company is coming for a long weekend, it all comes down to understanding hospitality. If hospitality doesn't come naturally to you, you can start simply with an open heart and an open door.

An Open Heart

Mark and I have always believed that the best way to know where your kids are is by making your home the place to hang. Doing this requires sacrifices on your part as a parent. There's emotional sacrifice when you are enjoying a quiet evening at home reading a book, and your teenager calls you after the football game and says, "Can we come hang at the house and watch a movie?" There's financial sacrifice when you know you need to feed whatever friends your son or daughter brings home with them. And then there's wear and tear on your home, your furniture, and your Xbox or GameCube.

But it's all worth it when you hear them laughing in the family room, playing Ping-Pong in the garage, or jumping on the trampoline in the backyard. It's then that you realize the benefits of knowing where your kid is and knowing you are providing a fun, safe environment for other kids as well.

Our friends the Anhalt's have a hangout home. Their kids' friends drop by at all hours of the evening and usually spend a huge quantity of time in their pool throughout the summer. Evan says he always feels welcome there. They started a unique tradition with the kids that have hung out at their house throughout high school. When it's your birthday, they ask you what flavor of ice cream you want and they special order it at www.Oberweis.com to be delivered to the Anhalt home. When it arrives, they call the birthday person and let them know their ice cream is waiting for them. This small act of kindness speaks volumes to each kid on their birthday.

When home is a hangout, the kids want to be in your home. They find it a fun place to be, and they feel comfortable enough to know your heart is always open and they are always welcome.

An Open Door

In Mexico it's said, "Mi casa es tu casa." In English, "My home is your home." If our home is to have an open-door policy, it starts by realizing that our home really doesn't belong to us. Everything we have belongs to God—He just asks us to be good stewards of what He gives us.

We hold our Hearts at Home management team meetings at my house most Monday mornings. As each person comes in for the meeting, they begin opening cabinets and pulling out glasses for ice water and mugs for tea and hot chocolate. Occasionally there's a request for a peanut butter sandwich when someone didn't have time for breakfast. I don't see that as an infringement of my privacy. Truly, my house is their house. One day a team member's car wouldn't start after our meeting and she needed to pick up her kids from school. On that day my car became her car. She jumped in and headed off to get her kids.

What makes a home a place people want to come to? What makes home a place the kids enjoy bringing their friends to? I believe four important elements make a home a hangout:

1. Emotional safety. If people feel they are walking on eggshells around family members, they'll opt to hang somewhere else. A hangout home has emotional safety that assures anyone who enters that they won't hear family members screaming and yelling at one another or sense unspoken anger or emotions. When I was in high school, one of my friend's father was an alcoholic who was often loud and angry, so her home was never a hangout. It wasn't emotionally safe.

2. Hospitality. When you walk into a home where someone has the gift of hospitality, you feel cared for and welcome. Hospitality is expressed in little acts of kindness, such as offering food and drink, showing people how to make themselves at home, and providing welcoming, interactive conversation.

3. Friendliness. If the people in the home show an interest in whoever walks in the door, "friendly" will be a word used to describe that home. A warm, genuine love for other people draws people into our home.

4. General cleanliness. While I hesitate to put this into our list of what makes a home a hangout, I do think it bears considering. We've all been in homes that are so cluttered or so dirty that you find yourself feeling stressed just being there.

On the flip side, a home doesn't have to look as though it could be featured in *House Beautiful* to make others feel welcome. In fact, an antiseptic home that feels cold and unlived in can be just as uncomfortable as a dirty home. What is needed is a balance between the two—lived in enough to be comfortable, yet organized and clean enough so that you don't have to worry about where you will sit.

If these four elements are present, our home is a place where people want to hang. Note that three of the four elements have nothing to do with the home, but rather with the people in the home. What makes home a hangout isn't about what the home has to offer, but rather what the people in the home have to offer to those who visit. Karen Ehman, in her book *A Life That Says Welcome,* helps define hospitality by clarifying how it is different from entertaining. She says, "Entertaining puts the emphasis on you and how you can impress others. Offering hospitality puts the emphasis on others and strives to meet their physical and spiritual needs so that they feel refreshed, not impressed, when they leave your home." She continues with, "Offering hospitality is much more about the condition of your heart than the condition of your home."[1]

It's important to understand that we're not talking about people taking advantage of us. We're talking about inviting others to make themselves at home. There is a difference. At the same time there are certainly boundaries that need to be considered.

Hospitality Boundaries

When home is a hospitality house, boundaries still need to be in place that help keep home in balance with all the other roles that home needs to play. Those who benefit from the open-door policy at your home need to also respect family time you might set aside.

At our home, Sunday night is family night. We've been doing that for many years. After church we all come home and take a nap or rest. Then we play together all evening: miniature golf, bowling, board games, popcorn and a movie—every Sunday is different. Because of this, the Savage home is not a hangout place on Sunday night. The kids' friends know not to stop by or call on Sunday nights because it's the Savages' family night and they have come to know and respect our traditions. Family friends don't ask us over on Sunday nights because they know we've already got plans. This is a boundary we've put in place to protect the other roles home needs to play in our life.

If you live in a neighborhood where your home is a hangout, you might try tying a bandana to your front doorknob when your children are not available to play. Then instruct the neighborhood children that when they see the bandana they cannot ring the doorbell or ask the children to play. The same could be done with a flag in the yard.

Another boundary to consider are personal capacity boundaries. For instance, I'm an introvert—that means that being alone fills me up. Mark is an extrovert—being with people fills him up. There are times that he wants our home to be a hangout and I just need a little bit of space. Maybe he wants to have some couples over on Friday night to play games, but I would rather be home alone all weekend with him and the kids. In that case he needs to respect my need for downtime and I need to respect his need for people. We might agree to having a quiet evening at home on Friday night and then having a few couples over on Saturday night.

Food, Glorious Food

Any kid who's been in the Savage home knows where our snack drawer is located. It's the top drawer right next to the refrigerator. One of the ways I make sure I'm ready for spur-of-the-moment hospitality is by making sure that drawer stays stocked.

Fruit snacks and goldfish crackers work well for the younger crowd, but bigger kids need bigger snacks. I've learned the value of keeping a stash of snack foods hidden in a place only I know about to pull out on impromptu movie nights following the football game. I also try to keep several frozen pizzas in the deep freeze for the times when the boys are hungry and chips and dip just won't do.

You don't have to go broke providing soda for every gathering.

Instead, keep lemonade mix on hand to fix at a moment's notice. A good supply of plastic cups and paper plates makes cleanup easier. When the cleanup is easier for me, it's like giving a present to myself.

During Evan's senior year one of his friends came over occasionally for a hearty breakfast of eggs, sausage, and toast. Now, I'm not much of a breakfast eater myself, so I rarely make a hot breakfast. My kids enjoy instant oatmeal or a bowl of cereal most mornings. But when Evan would ask if I would make him and Andy a hot breakfast occasionally and they would make the effort to get up early enough to enjoy it, I couldn't resist making home a hangout even in the early morning hours.

Thinking of Others

When we have a hospitality mind-set, we make decisions through a filter of thinking of others. When home is a place of hospitality, there's something to do for everyone. Kids of all ages like to be there. In order for this to happen, you and I have to think beyond ourselves and the needs of our families. We have to think about the needs of people God just might send our way.

Here are some ways to keep your home a place that says welcome to whoever might enter:

- After your kids are out of the baby stage, keep a bucket of baby toys in a place where they can be pulled out easily.

- As your kids enter the teen years, keep some classic toys such as Legos, building blocks, and Lincoln logs to entertain any grade-school visitors that might come over.

- Keep simple teen activities on hand such as Ping-Pong, soft-tip darts, and games like MadGab or Catch-Phrase, as well as several decks of cards.

- When your kids no longer need a stool to stand on in the bathroom, keep one nearby for little ones who might occasionally be at your home.

- Hang on to one or two sippy cups and bibs for the same reason.

• Keep snacks on hand for impromptu company or kids hanging at your house.

With an others-centered mind-set, we keep our home a place of hospitality.

Home as a Bed-and-Breakfast

A hospitality house moves from a hangout to a bed-and-breakfast when company comes for an extended stay. One of the best ways to make home a place that says welcome to overnight guests is to anticipate their needs.

When I spent a few days as a guest in my friend Janice's house, she showed me the room I would be staying in. At the foot of the bed was a basket she had prepared for me filled with all kinds of things I might need while I was staying there. It made such an impression on me I've tried to do the same for others when they stay at my home.

Some items to consider for a hospitality basket include:

• Small bottles of shampoo and conditioner

• Disposable razor

• Toothbrush and small tube of toothpaste

• Fruit (apples, bananas) and granola bars

• Chocolate kisses or a bag of M&M's

In addition to the above, make sure there is a box of Kleenex in the room, a towel-and-washcloth set, and a hair dryer available as well. When the kids have friends over, I don't make the fuss of a hospitality basket. However, I have learned to keep a 12-pack of inexpensive toothbrushes and a few travel-size toothpastes on hand for the child who inevitably forgot to pack her toothbrush for the slumber party. A little bit of forethought puts guests at ease and makes sure they feel right at home.

If you don't have a guest room, don't worry. Most of us don't have that luxury. This provides an opportunity for lessons in hospitality for your kids. You might have the kids alternate giving up their room for overnight company. You can even have the accommodating child help you assemble the hospitality basket to put in the room, giving them ownership of creating an inviting environment for your guest. In our home, the oldest child at home occupies the largest bedroom with an attached bathroom. When they move into that room, we establish that because they have the benefit of so much space and a private bathroom, they automatically relinquish their room as the guest room anytime we have overnight company.

It's possible that it really is best for visiting guests to stay in a local hotel simply because of the size of your home or your spouse's work schedule. If so, you can still say "Welcome" with a hospitality basket waiting at the front desk when they arrive.

Home Away from Home

When Anne was a toddler, I volunteered for our local Meals on Wheels program. Meals on Wheels provides one hot meal and one cold meal on a regular basis for elderly shut-ins. Each Wednesday I would drive to our community hospital to pick up my meals and a list of whom I was to deliver them to. Most people on the list were regulars that I began to build relationships with. They often looked forward to Anne's two-year-old grin and ready hug just as much as the food I delivered.

Not one of these people would probably ever set foot in our home, but we brought home to them. You might have an extremely small home or a spouse who doesn't share your desire for your home to be a hospitality house, but that doesn't have to stop you from having a heart that says, "Welcome to my world."

When home is a hospitality house, the hospitality can easily extend beyond the house. Your hospitality might take a new mom a meal. You might offer to watch the child of someone recovering from surgery. You might offer to go grocery shopping for an elderly neighbor or mow the yard for a single mother you've met at church. All of these are ways you can bring your hospitality to those around you.

Not everyone knows how to just step in and help. Sometimes

we need help thinking through options and some practical ideas for extending hospitality outside the home. When another mom can use a little bit of assistance, consider these possibilities:

Meals

When providing a meal for another family, there are a few things to keep in mind.

- Ask about food allergies and likes and dislikes, if you can.
- Steer clear of making food with ingredients that not everyone enjoys (for example, nuts, coconut, etc.).
- Tape clear instructions to the top of anything that needs to be tossed, baked, or warmed up.
- Use disposable containers so the family will not have the responsibility of washing pans, keeping track of whom they belong to, and remembering to return them to you.
- If the family has young children that Mom needs to feed at lunchtime, a sealed container or baggie full of premade peanut butter sandwiches can be helpful for her to give a hungry preschooler a snack or simple lunch.
- If you don't cook much yourself but want to provide a meal, you might give the family a gift certificate for pizza or Chinese food that they can order and have delivered to their home.

Laundry

Help with the laundry can relieve a weight from any mom who is under the weather.

- Go to the house and ask to take all the laundry home. Return it within 24 hours washed, dried, and folded.
- Offer to gather, sort, and start a load and help her fold any loads that were washed and dried but never folded. (If you put a load of dried, wrinkled clothing back in the dryer, spray them with water using a spray bottle, and then run the dryer for 15 minutes, most of the wrinkles will disappear.)

Driving

Most children need to be taken to school, piano lessons, or church activities.

- Offer to take the kids to and from school.
- Offer to chauffeur kids to lessons or activities they need to attend.
- Offer to go to the drugstore to fill prescriptions or get over-the-counter medication she might need.

Shopping

Eventually milk and bread runs out at home and someone needs to go to the store.

- Give the mom a call and ask what brand milk and bread she buys and offer to bring her the basic necessities. Just pick up her supplies when you are at the store for your weekly shopping.
- If she needs to pack lunches for her school-age children, give her the gift of convenience foods, such as Lunchables, juice boxes, or crustless peanut butter and jelly sandwiches (available in the freezer section) that can easily be thrown into a lunch box in the morning.

Housekeeping

Cleaning and clutter can get me down when I feel well. When I'm ill it's depressing to know that housecleaning needs to be done, but I lack the energy to get it accomplished.

- Ask your family member, friend, or neighbor, "Concerning your house, what is bothering you the most?" If it's the kids' toys spread all over the place, offer to pick up the toys. If it's a bathroom that needs to be cleaned or dishes that need to be washed, offer to clean. If it's a kitchen floor that she's sticking to every time she walks in the room, offer to mop the floor.
- Organize a group of friends to come in and do a one-hour

cleaning blitz of the house to really bless the person who's not feeling well.

Sometimes it's the simplest acts of kindness that can mean the most. When I was recovering from surgery, a friend called and said, "I'm within two blocks of Steak 'n Shake. What flavor shake can I bring you?" She brought the shake and stopped by for a short visit. When you take hospitality from your home to another home, it lets someone know you care.

Welcome Home!

Three years ago, Hearts at Home made our first trip to encourage moms in Europe. We took a team of 32 people to assist with the conference as well as other events we produced and participated in throughout a week. While there we stayed in a place known as the "Hospitality Haus." It wasn't a hotel; it was a ministry owned facility that slept about 35 people. Let me tell you—they lived up to their name. We experienced hospitality like never before. Each of us had our own twin bed and a bathroom we shared with a few others. There was a living room area where we could relax and watch a movie (although I don't remember having time to do that). While all of our food was prepared for us, the kitchen was always open. They explained cultural differences to us and made sure we understood how to use the public transportation. They truly worked hard to make us feel welcome in our "home away from home."

When home is a hospitality house, the goal is to make your home feel like "home" to anyone who enters. Whether it's watching someone else's kids, hosting an impromptu gathering of friends, or entertaining out of town guests, your home can provide a "home away from home" experience for all who enter.

When home is a hospitality house, I know I can extend a warm welcome to all who enter when I'm at home.

12

Home as a Cultural Center

Home is where your story begins.

ANNIE DANIELSON

My hands were bright red from the beet juice I was creating as I peeled and cut up more than a dozen beets. I remember eating beets as a child but not particularly liking them. Therefore, as a mother, I had not fed them to my family. Beets, however, are a staple food in Russia and one that Kolya loves dearly. The borscht I was making is a Russian soup that Kolya had often in the orphanage.

Not every family has the cultural opportunities that come with adopting a child from another country. All children, however, need to appreciate and celebrate the differences in others' skin tones, traditions, beliefs, food, and living environment. When home is a cultural center, it celebrates diversity and builds a heart that is accepting of others.

Know Your Family Heritage

"I remember when Brian and I first started dating that he asked me what nationality my family was," shared my friend Brenda. "I stuttered and stammered and meekly said, 'American?' Growing up in an Italian home, Brian naturally thought all families had a cultural element." Brian's family took a lot of pride in their heritage, passing along stories and traditions from generation to generation.

When I think of strong cultural family traditions, I think of my friend Diane. Raised in a bilingual home, Diane's family preserved their Polish heritage. When Diane became a mother, she continued the bilingual tradition. Her children all speak and understand both English and Polish. Her family often enjoys Polish cuisine. She has successfully blended Polish culture into their family's everyday life.

The first place to start making home a cultural center is with your own family tree. Does your family have a German background? Maybe a trip to a real German restaurant would introduce some German culture to your children. Do you have an American Indian heritage? Visiting an Indian museum or reservation could expose your children to some of the unique customs of Indian culture.

If your family knows little of its background, home can still be a cultural center by intentionally introducing your family to those who are different than they are. This can even be accomplished with some family field trips. A trip to a history museum will launch cultural discussions. If you have an Amish community near your home, a meal in an Amish home or a ride in a horse and buggy will do a great job helping kids see that others live differently than they do.

You don't even have to leave your home to introduce culture to your kids. Even as I'm writing this chapter, my kids are watching *Fiddler on the Roof.* Their interest was piqued when Erica performed in the musical at a local community theater. By watching it at home, I've been able to answer many questions that were raised in my sons' minds when they watched their sister's performance. We've talked about Jewish culture and traditions and how those enhance family identity and cultural heritage.

Be Missions Minded

She was just 15 when I watched Anne walk toward the airplane that would take her on her first international mission trip. Months earlier she had announced that she wanted to apply for *Brio* magazine's two-week mission trip to Venezuela (*Brio* is a Focus on the Family magazine for teen girls). To our surprise, she was chosen to be a part of the mission team. She didn't know one other person going on the trip; she simply had a heart for people who didn't know Christ.

Mark and I have always wanted our kids to be able to see beyond their little corner of the world. We've wanted them to have a heart for the hurting, a love for the less fortunate, and an ability to reach out beyond their middle-class suburban lifestyle. As parents we have found that we have to deliberately introduce our children to the world around them. Doing that requires creativity, intentionality, and a good measure of faith.

Anne is the oldest of our five children, and while missions seems to be a natural part of her heart (she has since traveled to China and several European countries), her siblings are still learning about the world around them and the opportunities they have to make a difference in the life of someone else. If you desire to help your children develop a mission mind-set, look for ways your family can reach out to the world around them:

- Choose a local mission organization where you can volunteer as a family. Work in a soup kitchen or volunteer to play games with the residents of a local retirement home. When our kids were younger, our family led the church service at a local nursing home—Mark preached, I led singing, one child played the piano, another read Scripture, and the youngest ones helped pass out hymnals and serve communion.

- Raise money together for a mission need. When we made the decision to adopt Kolya, we made the fund-raising a family affair. We found a project we could all work on together and saw God work in mighty ways as we raised thousands of dollars to make Kolya a part of our family.

- Sponsor a child through Compassion International. We allowed our children to help select a child for us to sponsor as a family. With three of our five children taking Spanish in school, they wanted to sponsor a Spanish-speaking child. We pray for him as a family and take turns writing to him. Compassion offers sponsor trips, and someday we would like to take our entire family on one of their trips to meet this young man we've "adopted" into our family.

- Take a short-term mission trip as a family. With each family member responsible for raising their own funds for the trip as well as stepping out of their comfort zone, they will learn life-changing lessons of sacrifice, prayer, mercy, and faith.

- Host an international student in your home. There are both short-term (two to four weeks) and long-term (nine months to one year) programs at the high school and college level. Your family will be blessed by the exposure to other cultural experiences, and you will have the opportunity to influence the life of a foreign student in some way.

- Let go and let God. When your junior high and high school children have an opportunity to take a youth mission trip or participate in inner-city mission work, don't let your fears get in the way of what God wants to do in their life. If they are willing to do the work and raise the funds, support their efforts in any way you can.

Opportunities to participate in mission work are around us every day. With just a bit of ingenuity, any family can turn their home into a cultural center.

Be Culturally Sensitive

"Buenos dios, Grandma Rosa." Those were some of the first Spanish words I learned as a four-year-old. Living in campus housing at Indiana University, my family was surrounded by people of different nationalities. I took a special liking to Grandma Rosa and her daughter, Rosina. Both Rosina and my father were finishing their doctoral degrees, and our families lived in the same apartment complex. I spoke just a few words of Spanish, and Grandma Rosa spoke only a few words of English, but that didn't stop us from communicating. I believe my exposure to different languages and traditions at an early age set in me a comfort level I would need later in life as I traveled to Russia to adopt our son.

When Mark and I found ourselves living in campus housing on

the Lincoln Christian College campus, we were able to afford our children a similar opportunity. Todd and Sandra lived next door to us. Sandra was Mexican and spoke little English. Todd, who was bilingual, had grown up in a missionary family serving in Mexico, where he and Sandra met. Todd and Sandra were newlyweds and didn't have children yet, but Sandra was a natural with kids. I hired her to help with my home day care during our years in Lincoln, Illinois. Because of this, both Anne and Evan heard Spanish spoken at a very early age. I believe that set a comfort level in place that Anne would eventually use to her benefit living overseas for three months in Paris, France. Other cultures and languages have never intimidated her as she has not only lived overseas but traveled to Venezuela, China, and Mexico on numerous mission trips.

We're never too old to learn about cultural differences. Several years ago I was asked to speak at a predominantly African-American event. I met many wonderful women throughout the day, and it seemed their conversations always came around to me being a "First Lady." One woman asked if I had met Beulah Mae. "She's a First Lady too," she said. Another woman approached me and said, "I understand you are a First Lady. Thank you for all that you do in that role." Honestly, I didn't know what these women were talking about. I'd smile and acknowledge their words, but I felt terribly intimidated by the unfamiliar term. I finally found the woman who had invited me to speak, pulled her aside quietly, and asked the $100,000 question. "Can you tell me what a First Lady is? It appears I am one, but I don't know what I am!" She laughed and said, "Why, Jill, a First Lady is a pastor's wife. You are a pastor's wife, aren't you? Then you are a First Lady." This was a term used in African-American culture and many African-American churches, but I'd never once heard it in my life. My cultural knowledge and understanding were expanded in that one moment.

Other Differences

Sometimes cultural differences have nothing to do with nationality or ethnicity. Somewhere along the way, our lives will inevitably intersect with someone with a physical or mental handicap. The more "normal" we can make those occurrences, the better for our children. If your family has the opportunity to befriend a special-needs child, it will be a huge blessing. Children need to see that physical or mental differences don't define a child; they are part of what makes him or her a unique person.

When I was in high school I had a part-time job caring for a wonderful woman. At the age of 40, Barbie had the mental capacities of a seven-year-old. She brought such joy to my life with her love for animals, her need for daily routine, and her nonstop conversations. I am so thankful for the chance Barbie gave me to rid myself of any intimidation about interacting with people different than I am.

Many times children and adults are unsure of how to relate to older people. They also seem like a different culture of sorts. If a child doesn't have the opportunity to be around older people, they may be intimated by their gruff voices, their walkers or wheelchairs, or even their bony, crippled fingers.

Our moms group used to have a once-a-week play day at a local nursing home. The kids would do puzzles and play games with the residents. The little ones would play ball or just play with toys and entertain the "grandmas" and "grandpas." It was a win-win for everyone involved. The nursing home residents loved the interaction with the kids, and the kids benefited from the time spent with older people.

The more kids are around people who are different than they are, the more it demystifies the differences. You'll have less staring, less intimidation, and less awkwardness when in the presence of those who are different than they are.

The Cultural Arts

Another aspect of culture we should consider in making home a cultural center is the cultural arts. The cultural arts include art, music, and theater. Most of the cultural arts are filled with history about people who live or lived in places different than us.

Classical music comes from a rich cultural background. Whether it's Russian symphonies from Tchaikovsky, German suites of Johann Sebastian Bach, or the American marches of John Philip Sousa, music brings culture alive to the ear.

Our daughter Erica loves the stage and has recently performed in *Fiddler on the Roof* and *Oliver.* Both experiences introduced her to vastly different cultures. She learned about the lifestyles of less fortunate people of another era. While the stories may be fiction, the culture they depict is accurate enough to introduce the performer or the audience member to circumstances different than their own. Our community theater opens every production with a "pay what you can" night. Without this, our family of seven would rarely be able to take in theater productions due to the ticket prices. You might see if your local theater offers a similar promotion to introduce your family to plays and musicals.

A trip to an art museum will open another world of culture. One can experience French impressionistic art or the artwork of Italy's Michelangelo. The artwork not only opens the door to culture, but to history as well. Culture is brought alive by learning about and experiencing the cultural arts.

I Accept You

Children need to learn at a young age that other people are different than they are. This world is a big place and filled with much diversity. An accepting heart will open a child up to cultural and relational experiences they might miss out on otherwise.

When a child is tolerant of differences and intrigued by diversity, their relationships and experiences will be richer and more fulfilling. The more they are around people whose customs are unlike ours, the more they understand the world they live in and marvel at the God who created us all.

When home is a cultural center, I know more about the world when I'm at home.

PART IV

The Personnel

13

Mom, Site Manager

The best occupation on the earth for a woman is to be a real mother to her children. It does not have much glory in it; there is a lot of grit and grime. But there is no greater place of ministry, position, or power than that of a mother.

PHIL WHISENHUNT

I became a mother just two weeks shy of my twenty-first birthday. Mark and I had been married a little over a year and a half when Anne came along. She entered this world as a double footling breech, and I found myself on an operating table having an unexpected cesarean birth.

My twenty-first birthday came and went without much celebration. I was moving slowly, still recovering from abdominal surgery. Engorgement had set in, and I felt as though my breasts were going to explode much of the time. Because Anne had her nights and days mixed up, I was operating on little to no sleep.

Welcome to motherhood.

My guess is that for you, just like me, motherhood surprised you somehow. Maybe it was how physically demanding it was. Maybe it brought out emotions you weren't prepared for. Maybe it was harder than you thought it would be. Maybe you were surprised how much you could love something so small and helpless. Many things surprised me when I became a mother, but one that stands out most in my mind was my discovery of just how important home was to me.

I was a full-time student when I gave birth to Anne. I took

off the second semester of my junior year for her entry into this world on a cold February morning. That summer, as I prepared to return to my full-time school schedule, I began looking at child care options. I didn't want her to go to someone else's home; I wanted her cared for in *our* home. Being home with her from February through August had planted a seed in my heart for the value of home. At that point in my life, however, the value of an education superseded the value of home. I eventually resigned myself that Anne would have to be cared for somewhere outside of our home until I finished my degree.

Seventeen months later Mark and I discovered that we would be adding another little Savage to our family. I completed my student teaching waddling to the front of the classroom every day, and had Evan on my graduation day.

Two months later we moved from Indiana to Illinois so my husband could pursue Bible College, and I found myself at home by default; I couldn't find a position to teach music at any school in or around Lincoln, Illinois. But God was using this "closed door" to water the seed He had planted more than two years ago. For income purposes, I began to watch other people's children in my home. When I became the day care provider, I saw the value of home in a completely different way.

After a move to Bloomington, Illinois, Mark and I decided I needed to be home until the kids were in school. That was a great idea except for the fact that we kept having kids. When Evan was in preschool, little Erica came along. As Erica was getting ready to go to kindergarten, Austin was born. And six years later, we added Kolya to our family through adoption.

Because of the spacing of our children's ages, I was a mother of a preschooler for 17 years! With my commitment to be home until the kids were in school, motherhood became my profession during that time. However, our youngest is now entering fifth grade and I'm still at home. "Why?" you might ask. "Because of the value of home," I would respond.

The Value of Home

It was Rose Kennedy who said, "I looked on child rearing not only as a work of love and duty but as a profession that demanded the best that I could bring to it." Like Rose, I have found that indeed motherhood is a profession, and it certainly deserves the best I can bring to it.

What happens at home is central to a child's ability to function throughout his life. Home is where bonding takes place and a child learns to attach to relationships. When a child can attach, that means they learn to trust people. Learning to trust is essential for having healthy relationships throughout life.

Our adopted son, Kolya, lived in an orphanage for the first nine years of his life. While it appears that it was a good orphanage, as orphanages go, the reality is that group care is never the same as mothering care. Since Kolya became a part of our family, Mark and I have been intentional about helping him learn to trust. Because I couldn't snuggle him as a baby, I've worked to snuggle with him in other ways. Sometimes I rub his legs, arms, and back with lotion at bedtime, other times we snuggle on the couch watching TV. This child doesn't need quality time; he needs quantity time. He needs to know that we're there in the morning when he wakes up and there at night when he goes to bed. He needs to know we'll be there after school and at any sport or music event he participates in. Home is where he is learning to trust, to love, and to be loved.

Home is where a child learns who they are. Each of us is created uniquely by God. We have unique gifts, talents, and temperaments. Home is the place those are discovered and celebrated.

Home is where we learn whose we are. We're not designed to journey through life alone. God created us to have relationship with Him. The most effective place for us to learn that is not at church—it's at home!

Home serves as our base camp. It's where we rest our head every night. It's the place we find clean clothes and a warm meal. It's a place of protection from the world and all that it demands.

With all the diverse roles that home plays in our life, someone has to be on duty to stay true to the construction blueprint.

On a construction site, the site manager is an on-site leader. He or she is present every day to make sure plans are followed, jobs are completed, and people are doing what they need to do. The site manager and the general contractor regularly communicate in order to keep the construction plan on task and on time. They confer and strategize together, and then the manager oversees the on-site work.

There is so much diversity in what goes on at home that an on-site manager is desperately needed. Someone needs to have the time and energy to invest in each member of the family as well as manage all the different facets of home. That's the essence of the job description for Mom, the site manager.

The Ministry of Availability

Dr. Swenson, in his book *Margin,* suggests that Christians need to have enough margin in their life so that when God asks them to do something, they are available to do it. He calls this the ministry of availability.

I'd like to suggest a slightly different perspective on that. I believe that motherhood *is* the ministry of availability. Our fast-paced world desperately needs people who recognize that life doesn't fit into nice little compartments of time such as: *this is when I'll work, this is when I won't work, this is when I'll take care of myself, this is when I'll play with my kids, this is when I'll spend time with my husband, this is when I'll talk with my kids...*I think you get the picture. Life doesn't work that way, and if we expect it to, we will find ourselves not only sorely disappointed but racked with guilt as well.

When Kolya jumped in the car after school and immediately asked, "Mom, who is my real mom? You know, the lady whose tummy I was in?" being available was of the utmost importance. His class had been discussing family trees in school that day, and his mind was swimming with questions that exploded out of him as soon as he left school. I needed to be available to answer those questions then—while they were fresh on his mind.

When my sister, who was pregnant with twins, ended up on full bed rest for more than three months, I had to be available: available to do her laundry, available to clean her house, available to take her older boys occasionally. But I couldn't do it all—her moms group stepped up to be available as well. Marilee spent one morning a week at her house asking, "What do you need done today, Juli?" Lianne organized women from the church to come and help do housework Juli simply couldn't do. Women from all over brought meals for months to help keep Juli in bed and keep those babies from being born too early. There was a whole band of women who stepped up because they believed in the ministry of availability.

Lotte Bailyn brought some perspective to this availability concept when she said, "Instant availability without continuous presence is probably the best role a mother can play." There is a balance between being there for your children and smothering them with your presence. Children need Mom to be available but not hovering over their lives in such a way that it robs them of independence and their ability to eventually fly from the nest.

Availability also doesn't mean that Mom is so focused on the needs of her family that she cannot take care of her own physical and emotional needs. Mom may be the site manager, but even a site manager has to step away from the job occasionally and take some time off. Who takes care of Mom? Mom has to learn the art of self-care.

The Art of Self-Care

I sat on the Southwest Airlines airplane with Anne on a trip to visit a pen pal in California. As we were preparing to push away from the gate, the flight attendant gave emergency and safety information. "Should there be a change in pressure in the plane, an oxygen mask will drop down above your head. Please place the mask over your mouth and nose and breathe normally." She continued with, "If you are traveling with a small child, please put your mask on first and then help your child with their mask. Oh, and if you are traveling with two children...well...you'll just have to pick your favorite!" Everyone on the plane laughed at her attempt to put humor into an otherwise monotonous message.

I've thought about those instructions many times since that trip. Not the part about picking your favorite, but the part where she said, "If you are traveling with a small child, please put your mask on first and then help your child with their mask." She was imparting wisdom to parents who would otherwise rush to the aid of a child before taking care of themselves. The principle behind the instruction is this: The best thing for the child in the long run is to have a parent who can take care of them beyond the crisis that requires the air mask. In other words, we need to take care of ourselves so that we can take care of our family. I believe that is a message every mom needs to hear.

No one else can do a better job at self-care than you. You have to identify the challenges of your job and strategies you can do to manage those challenges. You also have to identify what best refuels you emotionally and physically to help you go the distance you need to as a mom. Here are some common challenges that drain moms and some strategies for managing those challenges.

Isolation

When I first became a mom I couldn't believe how isolated I felt. I longed for a connection with other moms. I wanted to know if my experiences were normal and I needed to be with other women who understood what my life was like.

My friend Julie invited me to be a part of her playgroup. I jumped at the chance and found the camaraderie I was looking for. These women were just like me! This was my first introduction to the concept of a moms group, something I've been committed to ever since. Moms groups, whether small, loosely organized play-groups or well-structured community or church groups, are vital to a mom and her need to be with other moms. Every mom needs a mothering community—a place where she finds encouragement in her role as a wife and a mother. A moms group is also a place a mom can be cared for. When my sister went on bed rest with her pregnancy, her moms group was part of a community of women who took care of her in that challenging season. Who mothers the mother? Other mothers.

If you don't have a moms group, find one or start one. If you are a mother of a preschooler, you might start by looking for a MOPS (Mothers of Preschoolers) group in your area. Go to www.mops. org, type in your zip code, and you'll be given a list of groups near your home. If your kids are older or there isn't an established moms group in your area, you can start one of your own. You might want to pick up my book *Creating the Moms Group You've Been Looking For* at your local bookstore or at www.hearts-at-home.org to give you ideas and get you started in the right direction.

At the very least, start making an effort to spend time with other moms. Invite a mom and her kids over to play and visit. Ask a neighbor if she'd like to go out one night a week for pie and coffee. Be intentional about spending time with other women who understand what your life is like.

No Time Off

One of the biggest challenges of full-time motherhood is the fact that there's no lunch break, no vacation time, and you don't get to leave the office at the end of the day. In time, I found that this left me feeling both trapped and depleted. It's the repetitive monotony of "mommy tasks" that leave us longing for "just a few hours to myself." Can Mom have some time off? Absolutely! What she has to do, though, is learn how to create it for herself.

Time off for me has looked different in different seasons of my mothering journey. What has been consistent has been my strategy to find it. I learned early on that no one was going to walk up to me and say, "Jill, I think you need a break." Instead, I had to learn to build breaks into my life, ask for them clearly, and do whatever I could to make them happen.

When Anne and Evan were small, I attended an aerobics class three evenings a week. Asking Mark to cover the home front, I headed off for exercise, but even more than that I looked forward to the conversation each night. Most of the women enrolled in the class were moms, and our conversations before and after class were always encouraging.

When Erica was a baby, I longed to read the newspaper without interruption. That's when I asked Mark if he could give me 30 minutes each evening to read the newspaper in our bedroom. The time to myself was refueling. During that summer, I also asked Mark if one night of the week could be "Daddy night." He was agreeable to that, so after dinner each Thursday night, I would meet a friend for pie, shop, or head to a park with a blanket and a book.

When Erica was a preschooler, a friend and I discovered that we could give each other days off. We chose Tuesday as our day—one Tuesday was my day off and the next Tuesday was her day off. Our kids loved the arrangement because once a week they were assured of a play day together. Sometimes I would use my day off to simply come home and sleep, other days I chose to go shopping or run errands, and almost every time I would do lunch with my husband.

When asked what she wanted for her birthday, my friend Julie told her husband she wanted him to get her a hotel room just for herself. He obliged. On her birthday she checked into a local hotel with scrapbooking supplies in tow. She enjoyed a night to herself, watched any movie she wanted on television, and scrapbooked for hours. The next morning she woke up without the help of an alarm clock, had a leisurely morning, and checked out at noon. She said it was one of the nicest birthday presents she ever received!

If you haven't had time for yourself, think about the activities that would refuel you. Once you've determined your strategy, do whatever you need to do to make it happen. It will almost always require the help of other people: a sitter, your spouse, your parents, a friend, or a neighbor. The rewards are well worth the effort, however. You need it and your family needs it too.

Very Little Sense of Accomplishment

Most homemaking tasks could be described as mundane and repetitive. It takes four hours to clean up a house and only four minutes for your kids to trash it. A load of laundry takes two hours to complete and a potty-training toddler can dirty half that load in a single day. Once a meal is finished and all the dishes are washed or tucked in the dishwasher, it's almost time to be thinking about the next meal. At night after everyone is in bed, a weary mother can wonder, "Did I accomplish anything today?"

By the world's standards, it might not seem as though we have accomplished much. However, the world's standards don't apply to the profession of motherhood. In this profession, the little things are the big things: snuggling an infant, playing peekaboo, changing diapers, nursing, giving a bottle, attending tea parties with dolls, driving trucks in the sandbox, playing catch in the backyard, having a snack on the porch, listening to the saga of a teenage breakup, picking up a sick child from school…the list goes on and on. These are the accomplishments of motherhood. They can't be checked off a list. They don't earn you a raise. They are rarely measurable. BUT THEY MATTER A LOT.

You and I can't look for our sense of accomplishment on a daily basis. We have to look for it over the long haul…that's about 18 years or so. What I do today does matter, but it might not be noted or valued for a long time. Roy Lessin captures the essence of what a mother accomplishes in this poem that hangs on my wall:

CONTINUE ON
By Roy Lessin

A woman once fretted over the usefulness of her life.
She feared she was wasting her potential being a
devoted wife and mother.
She wondered if the time and energy she invested in her
husband and children would make a difference. At times
she got discouraged because so much of what she
did seemed to go unnoticed and unappreciated.

"Is it worth it?" she often wondered.
"Is there something better that
I could be doing with my time?"

It was during one of these moments of questioning
that she heard the still small voice of her heavenly
Father speak to her heart.

"You are a wife and mother because that is what I
have called you to be.

Much of what you do is hidden from the public eye.
But I notice.
Most of what you give is done without remuneration.
But I am your reward.

Your husband cannot be the man I have called him to be
without your support. Your influence upon him is greater than
you think and more powerful than you will ever know. I bless
him through your service and honor him through your love.

Your children are precious to Me.
Even more precious than they are to you.
I have entrusted them to your care to raise for Me.
What you invest in them is an offering to Me.
You may never be in the public spotlight.
But your obedience shines as a bright light before Me.
Continue on. Remember you are My servant.
Do all to please Me."

(By Roy Lessin. Courtesy © 2007 DaySpring Cards.
www.dayspring.com)

A woman in the profession of mothering serves and cares for her family as an extension of her relationship with God: "Whatever you did for one of the least of these…you did for me" (Matthew 25:40). With that perspective, there are no menial tasks, there is much accomplishment, and there is a higher sense of purpose. Understanding that perspective is the highest form of self-care there is.

The Art of Homemaking

The word "homemaker" is often considered passé. It brings about connotations of June Cleaver in the 1950s show *Leave It to Beaver.* Today's mom at home is known as a "stay-at-home mom," a "mother at home," a "domestic engineer," but rarely a "homemaker." However, before we completely throw this word out, I think we need to consider how appropriate it really is. The word "homemaking" is a beautiful word. It describes "a person who makes a home."

In *Professionalizing Motherhood* I quoted Holly Schurter, a mother of eight, on the concept of homemaking. I think her words bear repeating:

> Cultivate the skills, not only of housekeeping, but of making a home for your family. As you know already, they are not always exactly the same. Housekeeping consists of the laundry, the dishes, the toilets, and floors that need to be scrubbed, but homemaking is something else…
>
> Homemaking is the deliberate cultivation of beauty and productivity in family relationships. Homemaking is about helping your family feel loved and comforted. Homemaking is about celebrating each other, and about caring for each other, as well as for your friends and extended families and even the occasional stranger. Anyone can keep house. Not everyone bothers to make a home.[1]

Homemaking happens when we fully understand the value of home in our lives. Homemaking happens when we intentionally make home a safe house, a trauma unit, a pep rally, a playground, a school, and more. Somebody has to have the time and energy to bring those roles alive in a family's life. Somebody has to make a house a home. Homemaking is majoring in family relationships.

I think Laura Ingalls Wilder captured it best when she said, "Just as a little thread of gold, running through a fabric, brightens the whole garment, so women's work at home, while only the doing of little things, is just like the golden gleam of sunlight that runs through and brightens the whole fabric of civilization."

Aromatherapy at Home

Some housekeeping tasks contribute toward making a house a home. For instance, have you ever considered how important smells are for a family? It's amazing where your sense of smell can take you. One whiff of someone's perfume can bring to mind a special friend who used to wear the same fragrance. The smell of cookies baking will take you back to when you were grade school age and sitting in your grandmother's kitchen. Or the fragrance of fresh flowers can cause you to remember the first bouquet delivered to your door.

However, scents not only cause us to reminisce. Aromatherapy experts will tell you that certain smells aid in emotional wellness. For instance, lavender is supposed to ease anxiety, jasmine boosts confidence, and ginger fights fatigue. I don't know that I completely buy into all the claims of aromatherapy, but as a mother I have come to understand what smells in our home mean to my family and friends. It's really one aspect of the art of homemaking.

When the kids come home from school and smell cookies baking in the oven, they feel nurtured and cared for. No matter what challenges the school day brought, it fades at the smell of fresh-baked cookies.

When my husband comes home from work and dinner is cooking, he immediately feels that home is a safe place. A refuge. A place where he is cared for. Whatever stress was experienced at work begins to melt as he walks in and knows that food and comfort go hand in hand.

When a friend stops by and smells a pot of coffee brewing, she knows someone was anticipating her arrival. She feels welcome. There is relational warmth extended to her.

When my family comes home to the smell of Pledge or Lysol, they know someone has been caring for the home they live in. There's something about the smell of cleaning products that says, "Everything's okay at home."

Our home is designed to be a place where we can relax, find comfort, feel safe, and receive love. Smells can never substitute for quality conversation, physical affection, or words of encouragement, but they can have a powerful effect on our emotions and sense of security in the family unit.

Several years ago I heard author and speaker Elise Arndt, a mother of five, share some of the things she had learned about homemaking. One of the things she talked about was aromatherapy for the family. She shared her secret of boiling an onion on the stove when she didn't know what was for dinner. The smell of the onion soothed her and spoke volumes to the family because it said, "Dinner is cooking. Mom's got it under control. Life is okay." And it bought her time to figure out what to add to that onion to feed her family of six.

When I first heard her talk about spraying Pledge as an air freshener or boiling an onion, I thought it might be a bit deceitful. Then I thought about the fragrance of a burning "sugar cookie" candle or the smell of potpourri or melted wax chips. Many of us intentionally fill our home with the fragrance of our favorite candle or air freshener. Elise was simply creating her own scents to speak to the specific needs of her family.

One of the reasons I'm at home is to provide an environment my family wants to come home to. As best I can, I can create a welcoming, soothing atmosphere to speak love to my family. Personally, I really don't know if peppermint improves concentration, but what I do know is that occasionally the smell of a boiling onion does wonders for my mind-set and has an incredible calming effect upon our home.

It also buys me time to figure out what's for dinner...

The Power of Mother Love

The back cover of Dr. Brenda Hunter's book *The Power of Mother Love* casts a vision for moms:

> Mother love shapes cultures and individuals. While most mothers know that their love and emotional availability are vital to their children's well-being, many of us do not understand the profound and long-lasting impact we have in developing our young children's brains, teaching them

> first lessons of love, shaping their consciences…At a time
> when society urges women to seek their worth and personal
> fulfillment in things that take them away from their fami-
> lies and intimate bonds, Hunter invites women to come
> home—to their children, their best selves, their hearts.

I don't know that any of us grasp the power of mother love in a child's life. As we consider the importance of a mother's love, we might begin by looking at our relationship with our own mother. A mother's ability to nurture her children is greatly influenced by the nurturing she received herself as a child. If there was absence or emotional distance, there may be an emotional gap that needs to be closed for a mom to be fully available to her children.

You and I need to be willing to look inside our own experiences to identify any places we may still be affected by our relationship with our own mother. We can begin that journey by simply being willing to search our heart and better understand ourselves. Professional counseling may also be a valuable part of that process. Laura Ingalls Wilder said, "What is there in the attitude of your children toward yourself that you wish were different? Search your own heart and learn if your ways toward your own mother could be improved." This is important whether your mother is still living or not. You and I are deeply affected by our relationship with our mother and one of the most powerful gifts we can give to our children is our own emotional health. A first step you can take on this journey is reading *The Mom I Want to Be* by T. Suzanne Eller. This book is designed to help you rise above your past and give your kids a great future.

A child should never feel as if they need to earn a mother's love. This will leave a void in their heart all of their life. A mother's love needs to be given unconditionally to establish trust and a firm foundation of emotional intimacy in a child's life. If love is withheld, a child will look for it in a million other ways, sometimes throughout their lifetime unless they come to some sort of peace with their past. The emotional foundation we give our children at home is foundational to their life. We cannot underestimate the value of home and the power of mother love.

It's All About Influence

The profession of motherhood is all about influence. You and I have an incredible opportunity to influence the next generation by what we do as a mother every day. This is why intentionality is so important during the years that we raise our family. Be intentional about your own healing from life's hurts. Be intentional about taking care of yourself. Be intentional about investing in your marriage. Be intentional about parenting. Be intentional about homemaking. Intentionality increases influence, and influence is something God asks us to be intentional about. We cannot underestimate the power of mother love, the value of home, and the significance of our intentional presence in the home.

When Mom is the site manager, her heart, mind, and time are devoted to making home a place her family wants to be.

14

Dad, General Contractor

*My joy burns brighter when I tend to the glowing
hearth fires of home.*

THOMAS KINKADE

Tending the hearth fires of home is most often seen as a woman's job. I find it interesting that the quote at the top of this page comes from a man. It was Thomas Kinkade who identified that his "joy burns brighter when [tending] to the glowing hearth fires at home." The role of Dad in the home is far greater than most men realize.

On a construction site, the general contractor assumes responsibility for completing a construction project. He oversees the entire project—casting vision, setting strategy, and delegating leadership where it needs to be delegated. He may not be on-site at all times, but he monitors progress, sets direction, and stays fully involved through to completion.

Kids need a dad who is engaged and involved. They need vision for their future, direction for their decisions, and encouragement in their endeavors. They need Dad to serve as a general contractor in the process of building their lives and their future.

Be Fully There

Each evening Mark comes home to a regular routine. He comes in and greets everyone, heads upstairs to change clothes, and then it's 15 minutes on the couch. Mark's 15 minutes are a strategic part of his day because they allow him to get just enough of a nap to have the energy for his second shift: loving husband and involved father.

Kids need a father who knows who their friends are, knows what they are doing in school, and knows what they are struggling with in life. They need a dad who is fully engaged, fully there with his family. Because of that, Dad needs to know how to successfully transition from work to home. This reminds me of a story whose author is unknown.

THE WORRY TREE

The carpenter I hired to help me restore an old farmhouse had just finished a rough first day on the job. A flat tire made him lose an hour of work, his electric saw quit, and now his ancient pickup truck refused to start. While I drove him home, he sat in stony silence.

On arriving, he invited me in to meet his family. As we walked toward the front door, he paused briefly at a small tree, touching the tips of the branches with both hands. When opening the door, he underwent an amazing transformation. His tanned face was wreathed in smiles, and he hugged his two small children and gave his wife a kiss.

Afterward he walked me to the car. We passed the tree and my curiosity got the better of me. I asked him about what I had seen him do earlier.

"Oh, that's my trouble tree," he replied. "I know I can't help having troubles on the job, but one thing for sure, troubles don't belong in the house with my wife and the children. So I just hang them on the tree every night when I come home. Then in the morning I pick them up again."

"Funny thing is," he smiled, "when I come out in the morning to pick 'em up, there aren't nearly as many as I remember hanging up the night before."

Dad's transition from work to home may involve a nap or it might involve a "worry tree." I know some dads who stop at the gym on the way home to mark an end to their workday and transition into home life. Whatever the strategy, Dad needs to be intentional about making it happen so he can be there fully for his family.

Be Engaged

It was Valentine's Day when I received a call from Mark wanting me to confirm how to get to our oldest daughter's new place of employment. He had stopped by the florist and picked up a rose for each of our girls. His first stop had been the high school, leaving the flower for the school office to deliver to Erica. He was now on his way to drop one off at Anne's place of employment.

That simple act of kindness spoke volumes to our daughters. Their dad thought of them on a day when romance is celebrated. He wanted them to know that they were special and someone's special valentine.

An engaged dad is involved in his kids' lives. He is sensitive to their struggles, knowledgeable of their activities, and in tune with their hearts. Sometimes Dad needs Mom, who is on-site, to brief him about things on the home front. Sometimes he gets his information from one-on-one conversations with his kids.

Beginning in the infant stage, an engaged father changes diapers, gives bottles, and sees to baths. In the toddler years he pulls his son in a wagon, plays pat-a-cake with him, and reads him his bedtime stories. During the preschool years, an engaged father will wrestle with his kids, play Hi Ho! Cherry-O, and tuck them in bed at night. As the kids get older, a dad might take his daughter out on a regular date to show her that a man needs to treat a woman with care and dignity. He might set up a lunch once a week with his teenage son. They might share a sport together, such as bike riding or fishing.

Kids long to know their dad and for their dad to know them. To launch a conversation with his kids, a dad might start with questions like:

- What is your favorite part of the school day?
- What do you like to do best after school?

- Who are your best friends and why do you like them?
- If you could plan our family vacation, where would we go?

Time spent with Dad, whether it's "on a date" or playing catch in the backyard, is essential to a child's success in life. When a father is absent, either physically or emotionally, there are negative effects on a child:

- Problems with school performance
- Behavior problems at school
- Boys often score lower on a variety of moral indexes
- Problems with emotional and social adjustment
- More likely to choose deviant peers
- More likely to use and abuse illegal drugs, alcohol, and tobacco
- More likely to engage in greater and earlier sexual activity[1]

When a father is present, both physically and emotionally, there are great benefits for the child:

- Better academic achievers
- Better attitudes toward school
- Better overall life satisfaction
- Higher measures of self-acceptance and personal and social adjustment
- More likely to have positive peer relations and be well liked
- More likely to grow up to be tolerant and understanding
- Higher levels of moral maturity[2]

Kids need a dad who is involved, responsible, and committed. They need to know that he cares, he loves them unconditionally, and he is available when needed.

Be Free

Karen Ehman and Mary Steinke teach a popular Hearts at Home

workshop entitled "Let Dad Be Dad." These two moms address challenges moms face in letting Dad be free to be himself. I think Mary describes this best in her own words:

> The wild screams and uproarious laughter immediately drew me to the open window. What were my children up to now? And would the police be close behind?
>
> My wonderful husband, their entertaining dad, who should have been doing outside chores, instead decided to "hunt" down his children with his weapon of choice—the nozzle of a garden hose. Imagine three kids running in three directions, frigid water blasting, clothes sticking to shivering but smiling bodies, and their dad pursuing them around the yard with such focused abandon that it caused me to giggle.
>
> Then, in an instant, during a moment of inattentiveness, our oldest snatched away the nozzle and turned it on his dad, whose surprised pleasure at now being chased totally flabbergasted me.
>
> Their dad feigned the inability to outrun his three offspring. He "surrendered" by throwing himself on the ground, and all four boys wrestled on the ground until covered in mud and cut grass. What's a mom to do? Embrace their drenched dad and his antics. But wait until he dries off.
>
> Honest, I love fun. But my idea of water fun involves launching myself down the fast lane of the local waterslide. My kids love doing the water park with Mom, but they adore their dad's innate ability to clown around.
>
> I make dinner. He creates pancake masterpieces of a snowman, Mickey Mouse, or an "alien" (with so many melted M&M's in the flapjack that it looks disgusting).
>
> I read bedtime stories with expression. He reads using different character voices, making up the dialog, and completely changing the plot.
>
> When I play electronic games with our kids, I always crash and burn in the first 30 seconds. He devises new strategies, plays tournaments, and hollers the loudest when he wins.
>
> Now, I can't say that I have always embraced the amazing antics of

their drenched dad. I've been known to see the end result—more work for me, minor safety issues, or my kids learning things that I'd rather they didn't know, such as throwing a dinner roll across the room—before I see the parenting payoff of a stronger relationship with their dad.

Yet, I've discovered that letting Dad be Dad remains one of the best things a mom can do for her children. For when we let—or rather encourage—Dad to be Dad, we support a different type of hands-on parenting that makes marvelous memories.

The big "DUH" in parenting is that moms and dads parent their children differently by design. But somehow moms forget that fact when faced with a spouse who "didn't do it the way I would've, which is, of course, the only right way to do it."

Who says his way is wrong, moms? Instead, it's just different by design. For when a wife encourages her husband to parent in his own unique, fun style, everybody wins. Her husband enjoys his children, de-stresses, and relives his own childhood. The kids grow closer to their dad, make memories, and relish life.

Although a wise mom realizes that she may never volunteer to be a moving target in a game of drenched Dad antics, she will reap countless benefits in her family life when she "lets" Dad be Dad.[3]

Letting Dad be Dad is an important strategy we moms need to understand. Too many dads feel criticized by their wives rather than encouraged to be who they are with their kids. Dad will inevitably do things differently than Mom would—but that rounds out a child's experience. It blends the best of both parents to shape and influence a child into the person he or she will become.

Be Committed

When Dr. Willard Harley wrote his marriage book *His Needs, Her Needs,* he conducted a survey to discover the top five needs of a man in marriage and the top five needs of a woman in marriage. One of the top needs of a woman was something called "family commitment." Dr. Harley describes family commitment as "a responsibility for the development of the children, teaching them the values of cooperation and care for each other. It is spending quality time with your children to help them develop into successful adults."[4]

Children need a committed father—one who considers their needs and development when making life decisions. Family commitment could also be described as having a "family filter" on at all times when making decisions that would affect the family. Here are some scenarios to further explain family commitment:

- Dad has the opportunity to work overtime. It's optional and doing so would be a financial benefit to the family. However, if he works tonight he'll miss his son's last baseball game of the season. A dad who understands family commitment will forgo the overtime and head to the game.

- A father moves up the corporate ladder year after year. He receives great recognition and financial rewards. However, to continue moving up the ladder his family must relocate every two to three years. Family commitment would require a dad to take a serious look at the emotional development of his children and the toll these moves might be taking on the family.

- Dad has been offered tickets to a sports event he'd love to attend. It happens to conflict with the opening night of his daughter's musical. A dad with a "family filter" that allows him to filter his decisions through their effect on his family will let the tickets pass by and sit in the front row of that musical performance.

When kids know that Dad is committed, they have great security knowing they are a priority in his life. When a child senses "my dad chose me," they feel valued as a person. Kids need a dad who is committed to his marriage and his children.

Be Healthy

Kids need a dad all of their growing up years, so it's important for Dad to take care of his health—both physical and emotional. Dads need to take care of their bodies so they have the energy they need as well as the longevity they need to care for their family.

Exercise and healthy eating helps Dad feel better about himself. When he feels good about himself, he's a better husband and father. Sometimes exercise aids with that transition time from work to home. It might also be a dad's time to spend with a friend playing racquetball, basketball, or some sport he enjoys.

Sometimes Dad needs to pay attention to his own emotional health to allow himself to be fully engaged in fatherhood. If Dad came from a dysfunctional family, is an adult child of an alcoholic, or didn't have a father figure in his own life, there may be gaps in his emotional health that keep him from being the father he wants to be. Seeking help in the form of professional counseling is a sign of strength, not weakness. A dad may need to search his own past to be able to be fully present for his children.

Seeking out education in marriage and parenting also contributes to emotional health. We're never too old to learn, and most parents need some sort of continuing education to help equip them for the never-ending challenges of ushering children into adulthood.

What Every Dad Needs

Most men would not be able to identify their own needs, as they often let "emotional stuff" sit at the bottom of the priority list. But dads have needs too. There are some gifts Mom and the kids can give to Dad every day that don't cost a dime, but their value is literally priceless.

Admiration. Dr. Harley's study found that one of a man's top five needs is admiration. Admiring traits, talents, and accomplishments is powerful communication to a father. Admiration can be spoken or written. Most importantly, it just needs to happen on a regular basis. Dads need to be built up at home. Tell Dad what you admire about him.

Appreciation. Dads rarely get a thank-you for the things they do. Providing leadership, income, and taking care of the house and yard are some of the contributions many dads make to the family. A thank-you for everyday things means the world to him. Tell Dad "thank you" for the things he does.

Help. Is there a job Dad needs to do in the yard or around the house that you can help him with? It's always more enjoyable to do a task with someone else. Ask Dad if there is something you can help him do.

Love. What is Dad's love language? Is it quality time, physical touch and closeness, acts of service, encouraging words, or gift giving? Everybody gives and receives love differently. Make sure you are speaking Dad's love language and not yours. To learn more about love languages, check out the book *The Five Love Languages* by Gary Chapman. Tell Dad you love him today—in his love language!

Respect. Respect is the act of showing consideration and high regard for another person. When a man knows that his family respects his knowledge, his experience, and his decisions, he has been given an incredible gift. Give Dad the respect he deserves today and every day.

Time. Dad needs time for himself, time alone with his wife, and time with the family. Mom and the kids can be sensitive to his time needs and encourage him to make them happen. Give Dad the gift of time today.

Tribute. Last year I wrote a tribute to my father. I honored him for the things he taught me, for the memories I have from my childhood, and for the life of integrity he lives. He was overwhelmed with the words I wrote. If you have a little time, sit down and write your father or your husband a tribute.

Value. Dad needs to feel needed. When a new baby arrives, Dad can sometimes feel he's been moved to the back burner. When Mom and kids have so much going on in their lives, Dads can feel left out. Let Dad know he is important in your life and greatly needed by you.

The Power of Father Love

Dr. Kevin Leman reminds fathers, "You may *feel* 'indispensable' to your work, but you *are* indispensable to your family."[5] We must never underestimate the power of father love. A young girl will sometimes become promiscuous trying to make up for a lack of love from her father. A boy might join a gang when he's looking for male companionship and acceptance from other males. The lack of a father's love and attention has powerful implications for a daughter or a son. Just as a building can't be built without a general contractor, so a family can't be built without Dad playing the role he was designed to fulfill. Dad should never take lightly the role he plays in his children's lives. They need a man who is fully present, engaged, and committed. They need a father who is free to be who God created him to be.

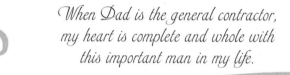

When Dad is the general contractor, my heart is complete and whole with this important man in my life.

15

Mom and Dad, Managing Partners

*A hundred years from now it will not matter what
my bank account was, the sort of house I lived in, or the kind of
car I drove. But the world may be different because I
was important in the life of a child.*

AUTHOR UNKNOWN

M ark and I sat down at our kitchen table after the kids were in bed
and began to discuss the coming week: Austin and Kolya were
starting school and needed some school supplies; Erica, preparing to
start her sophomore year in high school, needed school clothes; Evan
was moving back to Nashville, Tennessee, to continue his schooling
at Belmont University, and we needed to help him move into the
dorm; and Anne's wedding was just weeks away. Everyone was in a
time of transition, constructing new seasons of their lives. Mark and
I, as the managing partners of this construction job, had projects to
discuss and strategies to set to lead our family well.

The challenges of building a family are far longer lasting than
the challenges of building a house. However, the need to work in
partnership with one another is very similar. Mom and Dad need
to form a solid alliance as husband and wife in order to provide
strong leadership to the family for the long haul. They need to see
themselves as teammates working together toward common goals.

There are two primary goals Mom and Dad need to have: build a
strong marriage and parent well. Let's explore the implications of those
goals and how we can have a common vision keeping us on course.

Marriage First

My cell phone rang as I sat in the carpool line to pick up our son from high school. It was my husband calling from Arizona on his last day of a business trip. "What are you doing?" he asked. "I'm sitting in the carpool line at U-High." I responded. "Are you feeling spontaneous?" he asked. "Not particularly. Why?" I asked. "Because I was wondering if you would meet me in Chicago tonight. We could spend the night there and have a nice day together tomorrow."

Our conversation continued with me telling him he was crazy. It was 3:00 and I would need to meet his flight by 8:00 PM. It's a two-hour drive to Chicago from our central Illinois home, and I had four children to make arrangements for. Not only that, I was tired. After four days of parenting alone, I was almost too tired to think about one more thing.

Yet my own words echoed in my head. "You need to be a wife first and a mother second. Make your marriage a priority even in the midst of child rearing." That is a message I share with moms everywhere because I learned it the hard way after nearly destroying our marriage by making my children the priority over my husband.

So I relented. It struck me that our oldest daughter was often hired by families to babysit overnight; she was certainly capable of taking care of her siblings. I asked Anne to cover the home front, and she happily complied. But her youngest brother wasn't so agreeable.

As I threw a suitcase into the back of the car and gave everyone last-minute instructions and kisses, Austin began to cry. "Mommy, don't leave. I don't want you to leeeeeeaaaaave!" This was common for Austin, who has been a clingy child all of his life. At this moment, however, it really tugged at my heartstrings.

I hugged him and reassured him that his sister would take good care of him. Then Anne peeled him off my body and I slipped into the car. As I was driving out the driveway in tears, God brought another part of my day to my mind. That morning I had taken Austin to the doctor for an annual checkup. Upon learning that he was due for some shots, Austin began a similar petition. "Mommy,

I don't want any shots. Please don't let them give me any shots." Immunizations are a common fear for children, but as parents we certainly don't let their tears and fears jeopardize their health. We help them find their courage and sometimes hold them (against their will) so they can receive the protective immunization. We know what's best for them, but they don't always understand that.

This situation was the same. Sometimes what's best for a child is for a mother and father to spend some time together—just the two of them. Tonight that was what was best for Austin. I knew that, but he couldn't possibly understand that. It was my job to do what was best for him. Mark and I had been two ships passing in the night for the past month or so. We desperately needed time together—time to reconnect, laugh, and talk without interruption.

The absolute best parenting strategy you and I can have is to make our marriage a priority. This gives our kids the security they long for. In a child's world there is Mom and Dad. If Mom and Dad are okay, their world is okay.

If you and your spouse stopped dating when you said "I do," you may be finding there is distance between you. That distance can begin to close with some intentional investment in your marriage. You might want to reinstitute dating into your relationship.

First start with daily dates. A daily date is a phone call in the middle of the afternoon saying, "I was just thinking about you and wanted to check in." It's a cup of coffee out on the porch after dinner, talking for 15 to 20 minutes—just the two of you. Daily dates make sure you are connecting and communicating on a daily basis.

Then there are weekly dates. Weekly dates are the regular time you set aside to be together without kids. It might be weekly or biweekly, but the most important thing is that it is regular. Maybe you choose every other Friday night as your date night. Once you determine when it is, get it on the calendar, arrange for a sitter, and protect that time fiercely. Mark and I have our date days on Fridays because he's off on Fridays and our kids are in school. We spend every Friday together during the school year. During the summer we move our time to Friday night.

A date can be something as simple as a walk on a nature trail, gazing at books at a bookstore, or coffee at a quaint little coffee shop. It might be playing golf together, browsing antique stores, or watching the stars. It doesn't have to cost money. It just needs to be something you do together that fosters communication and includes a fun factor of some sort.

The final kind of date we need is an annual getaway. At the very least, take one night away to celebrate your anniversary. Did you know that if you saved just $10 a month from one anniversary to the next, you would have enough money for one night at a bed-and-breakfast? If going away doesn't work for you, have the kids spend the night somewhere and enjoy a night alone in your own home. Mark and I have found it beneficial to spend two to three nights a year away and every three years or so we take a one-week vacation for just the two of us. This always rejuvenates us and helps us stay focused on our relationship. Dating keeps us connected, invests in our relationship, and keeps the romance alive.

Revive Romance

"That was the most romantic thing you've ever done for me!" Those were the words I uttered when I stepped out of the airport to find my husband waiting to pick me up in the pouring rain. My car was in the airport parking lot, but when it began to rain hard, Mark had decided to drive to the airport, pull up to the curb, load my luggage into his car, and drive me to my car in the parking lot. It was an act of kindness that spoke volumes to me.

Mark responded that he didn't think of it as romance. "Romance is flowers, chocolates, love letters, and long walks on a beach," he replied. "Picking you up so you didn't have to walk in the rain isn't romance." I disagreed.

In fact, that small act of kindness prompted a new awareness in our marriage about what true romance really is. In the beginning of a relationship, romance consists of small acts of kindness as a man and a woman are getting to know one another: a love letter tucked into a mushy card, flowers for no reason, a box of chocolates on occasion. As the marriage matures, the same acts of kindness are needed, but they become more personalized as we grow to know one another.

Now, don't get me wrong. I still love flowers for no reason, and a love letter from my husband always melts my heart. However, I believe that real romance in a marriage comes from the little acts of unselfish kindness a "home management team" gives each other on a daily basis.

What is real romance? Here are some ideas to get you started:

- Turn on your spouse's electric blanket or heated mattress pad 30 minutes before he or she heads to bed.
- Offer to give baths and tuck the kids in bed when your spouse has had a hard day.
- Empty the dishwasher or do the dishes without being asked.
- Pour your spouse a cup of coffee or tea in the morning and bring it to the bathroom while he or she is getting ready.
- Assist with the grocery shopping on occasion.
- If she goes to the store alone, unload the groceries out of the car for her and put them away.
- Leave a love note on the mirror with lipstick or shaving cream.
- Open her car door.
- Prepare his favorite dessert.
- Surprise your spouse by cleaning and vacuuming his or her car.
- Tell her that you appreciate her and the things she does for the family.
- Tell him how much you appreciate how he provides for the family.
- Leave him a love note in his briefcase.
- Call her in the afternoon to check in and say "I love you."

- Take the children for a couple of hours to let her have time to herself.
- Forgive her.
- Forgive him.
- Listen to your spouse...really listen with your eyes and body language.
- Hold her hand or put your arm around her in church.
- Give a back rub.
- Buy his or her favorite candy bar or magazine when you stop to fill up your gas tank.
- Go to a ball game with him.
- Take in a "chick flick" with her.
- Massage his or her feet.
- Scrape the windows on her car after a frost or snow.
- Compliment your spouse publicly.
- Hire a sitter so the two of you can be alone on the weekend.
- Fill up your spouse's car with gas when you drive it.
- Praise your spouse in front of your in-laws.
- Give a hug...a big hug.
- Invite your spouse to cuddle while watching television.
- Take a half day off for just the two of you.
- Join your spouse in a hobby.
- Fold and put away the laundry.
- Have a cup of coffee or a glass of tea waiting when he or she comes home.
- Warm up the car for her.

My friend Brenda shared, "I find that if I do something that normally falls under my husband's area of responsibility, he really appreciates it. For example, if I take out the garbage, mow the lawn as a surprise, or do anything he usually does, he is grateful for the fact that he doesn't have to do that particular task. And it works that way for me too. If he cleans the bathrooms for me…WOW! I feel loved!"

She gave another example: "The other day he had to go to a class before he went to work. After he had left, I noticed that he forgot his phone at home. I obviously couldn't call him, but I did know where the class was, so I went and found his car. I put the phone where he could find it and left a note on his seat. You would have thought I had given the man one of my kidneys! The fact that I was thinking of him and did what was a small act of kindness spoke love loud and clear."

It is true that actions speak louder than words, especially in marriage. Telling your spouse that you love them is very important, but showing them your love will give credibility to your words. Unselfish acts of kindness—the true essence of romance—say "I love you!" without ever uttering a word. But is romance all there is? What about the sexual relationship in marriage? With kids in the picture, managing partners need to set some strategy in their physical relationship too.

Schedule Sex

The young mom on the other end of the phone poured out her frustrations. She desired sex, but her husband couldn't care less. As the parents of five, all under the age of six, they rarely found time for each other outside the bedroom, let alone inside. She confessed that she felt they were more like roommates than lovers.

I listened with understanding. As a mother of five myself, I know the struggle of keeping our family marriage centered, not child centered. I know the difficulties in finding time for just the two of us. And I know the challenge of differing sexual drives.

When she finally paused to catch her breath, I explained some of the strategies Mark and I found to keep our marriage a priority. We talked about creative date ideas, inexpensive child care options, and the importance of connecting on a daily basis. I asked her if she and her husband ever considered scheduling their sex life. She responded with an awkward silence.

Finally she laughed and said, "You're kidding, right? Sex is supposed to be spontaneous. Nobody *schedules* sex."

For 22 years of marriage, Mark and I have been at opposite ends of the spectrum when it comes to our sex drives. Mark thinks about sex once every 17 seconds. I think about it once every 17 days. And this wasn't our only marital challenge. Eventually we found ourselves in a marriage counselor's office.

Our differing sex drives were just one issue of many in our hurting relationship. During that healing season, we learned some new strategies for communication, conflict resolution, and compromise concerning our sexual differences. That's when we first discovered the concept of scheduling sex.

At first, just like that young mom, we couldn't get past the misconception that sex isn't something to be scheduled. But who says sex should always be spontaneous? Movies, television shows, magazine articles, and romance novels, that's who!

If we're not careful, we begin to use the media to determine what's "right" or "normal." But then, we're using the wrong measuring stick. We can't allow our culture to set direction for our relationship. Instead, we need to apply our God-given creativity to find the time and set the strategies to make our sex life within marriage work.

Once we were able to grasp that scheduling sex wasn't such a crazy idea, we put it into place within our partnership. Today, we're still amazed at the transformation it brings to our physical relationship.

How does planned lovemaking benefit a marriage? Consider these advantages.

It Eliminates "The Ask"

In most marriages, one partner possesses a higher desire than the other and requests sex more often, while his or her partner rarely asks for physical intimacy. For the spouse with a higher desire, the fear of rejection often sets in. One becomes weary of having to ask, or even beg, for sex on a regular basis.

When a couple can agree upon a basic schedule for sex in marriage, it takes the guesswork out. While this still leaves room for occasional spontaneity, it reassures the higher-sex-drive mate that it will happen, and not only that—they know *when!* Usually the schedule is less often than the partner with a higher desire would want and more frequent than the partner with a lesser desire may want, but it's meeting one another on middle ground.

It Increases Desire

For the partner with a diminished desire, scheduling sex engages the brain, the largest sex organ in the human body. The brain needs to be clued to prepare the body for a sexual response. Most people who have a lower sexual drive simply don't think about sex very often. Scheduling jump-starts this process.

Once sex is on the calendar, it provides a reminder to think about sex, prepares us mentally for being together physically, and primes us to "get in the mood." When I complained to a friend about having trouble getting in the mood, she said, "Jill, you're trying to go from making meatloaf to making love in 30 seconds flat? You can't do that. You have to have a strategy for going from point A to point B."

Rarely does the partner with a higher desire need to get "in the mood." In contrast, the partner with a lesser desire may need to work at it. When sex is on the calendar, though, it serves as a prompt to set strategies in motion. Scheduling sex reminds spouses that they're working together toward the goal of intimacy, valuing their appointed rendezvous, and doing whatever it takes to make it happen.

It Increases Anticipation

When lovemaking is kept on the front burner, it builds anticipation. Both husband and wife begin to prepare for their marital recreation. Have you ever thought of sex as recreation? It is! God gave us the gift of sex as a form of recreation in our marriage. It's our own private playground where God intends for us to enjoy physical pleasure.

When sex is on the schedule, we enjoy planning our time together because we both hold the same goal. We can even become a life-long learner of giving pleasure to each other. Keeping a couple of Christian sexual technique books on the shelf may develop us into connoisseurs of giving physical pleasure to each other, and it builds anticipation as we think about the next time we'll be together.

It Allows for Prime-Time Planning

He prefers nighttime when he can be romantic. She prefers daytime when she's not so tired. They decide that twice-a-week lovemaking is on their calendar—Tuesday at noon (he comes home for lunch and she arranges a sitter for the kids) and Friday at night (after a warm bath and an evening of watching a movie together or going out on a date). This schedule worked well for one couple we mentored.

Most couples not only differ in their desires concerning frequency of sex, but also in the atmosphere that's conducive to sex. Some struggle with making love anytime children are in the vicinity. Others prefer a certain time of the day. When you put your lovemaking on the calendar, you can work together to accommodate those likes and dislikes in order to meet the needs of both.

It Helps Couples Prepare Physically

I used to tease my husband that once we got on a lovemaking schedule, it sure took the pressure off shaving my legs every day! On a serious side, there's value in preparing yourself physically to make love to your mate. A hot bath or shower, a freshly shaved body, and some great-smelling lotion often relax us for physical intimacy. It also builds anticipation as you prepare to be with your spouse.

If weariness keeps you from being excited about sex, an early evening nap may be just the key if lovemaking is on the agenda that night. Since some of the guesswork is out of the mix, we can prepare not only mentally, but physically.

It Builds Trust

If we're going to commit to lovemaking on a regular basis, we need to honor our word and agreement. When we honor our word, we build trust and deepen intimacy. On the rare occasion that something prevents your regularly scheduled lovemaking, spouses need to communicate their value of sexual intimacy so they can make alternate plans to meet those physical and emotional needs. This is the key to successfully calendaring your intimacy.

Several weeks after that initial conversation, I spoke again with that young mom. Her voice held enthusiasm I hadn't heard before. I asked her how things were going, and she indicated that she and her husband were working on some new ways to energize and invest in their marriage.

She concluded by saying, "Now, don't bother calling Friday around noon, because no one is going to answer the phone!" I knew that she learned the same secret we learned years ago. While spontaneous sex may have its place in life, scheduling sex always has its place on our calendar!

Protect Your Marriage

The young mom chatted with me after a Hearts at Home conference. "Have you ever thought about having a conference for stay-at-home dads?" she asked. "There's a stay-at-home dad in our neighborhood who's become my best friend. We take the kids to the park, shop, and even do our once-a-month cooking together. He's a great guy!"

Sirens, whistles, and red flags went off in my head. I wanted to scream, "No! Don't be naive. Remove the blinders! Put boundaries in place and build a hedge of protection around your marriage!" It was obvious she had no idea about the danger of this seemingly harmless situation. As managing partners, you and your spouse need to set some strategy to protect your marriage.

Mark and I spend countless hours mentoring hurting marriages. We counsel others based on our own "back from the brink" experience many years ago when our marriage seemed hopeless. Many of these couples are dealing with damage caused by infidelity. The story is always the same: the unfaithful spouse develops a relationship that started as an innocent friendship. It was someone to talk to who listened and cared.

We know that story all too well. Even though no lines of unfaithfulness were crossed in our marriage, at the most difficult time of our relationship, I experienced an attraction for a man I worked with. Luckily, I realized the dangerous place I was in and got honest with Mark. We recognized the need for establishing boundaries in our personal lives that exist specifically to keep temptation at bay.

The Bible tells us that "each one is tempted when, by his own evil desire, he is dragged away and enticed. Then, after desire has conceived, it gives birth to sin; and sin, when it is full-grown, gives birth to death" (James 1:14-15). Temptation, enticement, desire, sin, death…those are the steps infidelity takes. Because of that, we have to put boundaries in place that keep us from stepping into situations where temptation can take place.

As we talk to hurting couples about advance decisions needed to protect our marriages, we use the line of trees along the west side of our house as an example. The previous owners had wisely planted the trees to provide a hedge of protection against the winds that rage across the cornfields. In the same way, we need to plant a hedge of protection around our marriage. That is, we need to make advance decisions that will keep temptation at bay and the marriage a priority.

Hedge 1: Choose wisely. Avoid unnecessarily spending time with someone of the opposite sex. For instance, if you're looking for a personal trainer at the local gym, choose someone of the same sex.

Hedge 2: Share carefully. If you find yourself sharing things about yourself or your marriage that you haven't or wouldn't share with your spouse, that's a red flag. Not all affairs are physical—an emotional affair is just as damaging.

Hedge 3: Stay in large, public settings. Determine not to meet one-on-one with anyone of the opposite sex. If your coworker asks if he or she can join you for lunch, ask a third person to join you as well. If necessary, don't hesitate to share the boundary you and your spouse have agreed upon in your marriage. You just might lead by example.

Hedge 4: Don't be naive. Most people who end up in affairs don't set out to have one. Infidelity usually begins with an innocent relationship that, in time, moves to an emotional depth that crosses a line of fidelity.

Hedge 5: Increase your investment at home. Solid marriages are built by spending time together, laughing together, and playing together. If you aren't dating your mate, set up dates for the coming months and make spending time together a priority.

Hedge 6: Pay attention to your thought life. When all you think about is your spouse's faults, any other man or woman will look better. Make a list of the strengths that initially attracted you to your spouse. Increase encouragement and decrease criticism.

Hedge 7: Don't play the comparison game. We all make mistakes, have bad habits and annoying behaviors. When we compare a "new friend" to our spouse, it's an unfair comparison because we aren't seeing that person in a "living under the same roof, taking care of kids at 3 AM, struggling to make ends meet" reality.

Hedge 8: Stay away from pornography. Viewing pornography is an affair in itself. Don't let your mind be drawn from your spouse. If pornography is a struggle, seek out both filtering software and accountability. Check out www.xxxchurch.com for more information.

Hedge 9: Don't get isolated. When we isolate ourselves, we detach from our environment. Isolation causes us to lose perspective and cuts us off from any natural accountability.

Hedge 10: Seek help. Seeking help is a sign of strength, not weakness. A counselor can provide valuable perspective and help set new strategies for a marriage that can go the distance.

When the hedge of trees was planted on our property, each tree was planted individually. As the trees grew in size and strength, they worked together to protect our home from unpredictable weather and wind. Each hedge we plant around our marriage will do the same. Each time we make a decision to protect our marriage, we are on our way to building a marriage that is marked by faithfulness and on its way to lasting a lifetime.

Partners in Parenting

It was Lucius D. Clay who declared, "Much is being said of the present crisis in the world and the need to do something about it. But to play a part and do our duty, we do not need to be the principal actors. We have only to be good citizens, good neighbors and—most of all—good parents." Those words were spoken well over 50 years ago when Mr. Clay served during the Eisenhower administration, but they ring true even today.

Being intentional as a parent is one of the most powerful ways we can not only serve our country, but impact the world as well. Many of the evils of our world are a result of a lack of nurturing in the life of a child. That's how important our role is as parents. Dr. Kevin Leman puts it this way:

> Parents—not drugs, not movies, not peer groups—are a child's number one influence...In a culture in which we complain about all the influences on a child's life, it's important to remember that parents *are* what make the difference. Your word, your silence, your presence, your absence, your example—both good and bad—all matter more in the life of your child than you may ever realize.[1]

When Mom and Dad are successful managing partners in parenting, a child grows up in a secure, stable environment that will equip him for life.

Love and Nurture

When Mark and I show affection for one another, our kids will often call for an "Oreo cookie hug." In an instant Mark and I become the chocolate cookies on the outside and they become the yummy filling on the inside as we squeeze together to give them a mom-and-dad hug. Sometimes another child will yell out "double stuff" and join in the fun.

Kids need to receive physical affection, love, and encouragement from parents both individually and together. There is something very powerful that happens when a child hears Mom and Dad say, "We're so proud of you." "We love you so much." "We thought you did a great job!" The "we" statements form a strong, united voice that speaks volumes to a child's heart, soul, and mind.

Occasionally Mark and I take one child out to dinner all by himself or herself. We use those opportunities to listen intently as they talk, giving them our full attention. We also try to speak words of encouragement that build them up as an individual. This helps us move from "group parenting" to individually loving and leading each child.

Another way to give children attention as a couple is for both parents to sit on their bed at night, listen to prayers, and tuck them in with a word of encouragement. If your kids are teenagers you no longer tuck in, engaging in conversation with them together anytime it's possible is valuable.

Establish Authority

Kids long for boundaries in their life. They'll always push the boundaries—which is the biggest challenge of parenting—but they secretly want them in a desperate way. When a child becomes their own authority, there's a silent message they begin to believe: "Nobody loves me enough to set limits."

Erica came home from musical practice at school one afternoon and blurted out, "Mom, you won't believe the conversation I had with this girl and her mom. The mom was working backstage and her daughter asked if she could do something after practice. The mom said no and they began to argue—not a bad argument, kind of half arguing and half teasing. Then the girl flipped her mother off! Do you know what the mom did then? She looked at me and said, 'Can you believe she can do that?'"

Erica was absolutely floored that this mother had allowed her daughter to act with such disrespect. She said, "Mom, the only reason she can do that is because her mother allows her to do that.

That's so sad." Yes, it is sad and far too many parents abdicate their role as an authority and let their kids call the shots—not only during the teen years, but even during the toddler and preschool years.

When Anne and Evan were ages six and four, we had a terrible time getting them to stay in bed. It was a battle every night. Mark and I were worn out and decided to ask a couple in the church who were past the preschool season of parenting to help us out. We respected them as parents and felt they could give us some direction. We asked them if they would be willing to come over one evening to witness the bedtime routine. They spent the evening with us and after the kids had been in bed and out of bed several times they said simply, "Guys, the problem is who's in charge. Your kids are calling the shots. You're not."

They were right. We were threatening punishment, but that's all we would do. We raised our voices and became frustrated with them, but we were never really in charge. With the help of our friends, Mark and I came up with consequences for getting out of bed that we were willing to enforce. The next day we sat the kids down and told them that from this point on they would be expected to stay in bed after we tucked them in. Then we stated what the consequences would be for the first time out of bed, the second time, etc.

It took only one week to turn things around. We made sure we were consistent with the consequences we had established, and both Anne and Evan saw that we meant business. By the end of seven days, we would tuck the kids in and then have a quiet evening to ourselves without an hour of bedtime battles. We had to learn how to be the authority in our children's lives.

In her book *Be the Parent*, Kendra Smiley shares this wisdom: " 'I am the parent. He is the child.' I said those two sentences more than once as we were raising our kids. Who was I trying to convince? Probably both of us, myself and my child. Actually, it was more of a reminder—a reminder I needed when there had been a mysterious role reversal. Saying, 'I am the parent. He is the child,' helped me restore each one of us to our proper place."[2]

What does being an authority look like? For some of us, the word "authority" brings about negative connotations because of abuses of authority we have experienced ourselves. One mom equates authority with raising her voice. "That's the only way the kids know I'm serious." Another parent feels that authority can only happen if you withhold nurturing and affection. "If I'm soft, they'll think they can get their way." Both of these perspectives are inaccurate pictures of authority.

Authority is a balance between giving both instruction and accountability. When there is a balance between these two entities in a loving environment, trust and respect are built. We all need healthy authority in our lives, and kids need to experience that with their parents first.

How do we establish authority? Here are five principles to follow:

1. Say what you mean and mean what you say. If you're likely to overreact or exaggerate, your kids will soon learn to not take you seriously. Measure your words carefully, and if you give an instruction, do not let it be an option.

2. Do not end your instructions to your kids with the one-word question, "Okay?" While most of us do this to get a response from our child to confirm they are listening, it subtly sends a message that the child has an option in obeying. "Johnny, it's almost bedtime. In five minutes I need you to begin to pick up your toys" works much better than, "Johnny it's almost bedtime. Begin picking up your toys, okay?"

3. Teach your children to give you a verbal response, such as "Yes, Mom" or "Yes, Dad" anytime you give them an instruction. This eliminates your need to insert an "okay?" at the end of every instruction to get a response out of them.

4. Expect obedience the first time and give an immediate consequence if it doesn't happen. When kids know you are

serious about accountability, they will begin to respect it
and expect it.

5. Be consistent. If there's even the slightest chance they can
   get away with disobedience, they'll take the risk and try.
   This results in a role reversal, where they call the shots rather
   than you.

Present a United Front

Mark and I have disagreed on a lot of things over our 21 years
of parenting. But the one thing we have always agreed upon is the
need to present a united front. The only way we can do this is to
handle our disagreements behind closed doors.

Marriage is the merging of two lives into one. That's a challenging task, to say the least. It requires the merging of traditions,
experiences (both good and bad), parenting styles, conflict management skills, expectations, philosophies, and more! We're bound
to disagree on how to handle parenting challenges that arise along
the way. So the first step in presenting a united front is to expect
disagreement.

Expecting disagreement helps with being proactive as a parent
rather than reactive. If at all possible, work to be ahead of your
children on how you will handle things like: extracurricular activities, jobs, driving privileges and responsibilities, paying for college,
etc. If you discuss these things ahead of time and agree upon what
freedoms and boundaries you will expect when the time arrives,
you'll be on the front end to lead your children rather than on the
back end trying to regain lost ground. We can't be perfect, but we
can be prepared.

Discuss and agree upon acceptable consequences for your
family. Is spanking an acceptable consequence? What other consequences are acceptable forms of accountability? Time-outs? Losing
privileges? Losing screens (TV, computer, video games)? Natural
consequences?

When Mom and Dad present a united front, it usually requires cooperation. Both Mom and Dad have to be willing to give a little in their perspectives and meet somewhere in the middle. That's much easier to do when discussing things proactively rather than reactively. If at all possible, work to be ahead of your kids.

Even the most prepared parents will still find themselves with a parenting dilemma that demands their attention. There have been many times that either Mark or I have been standing in the kitchen dealing with a situation with one of the kids. We send the child to their bedroom and then one of us says, "Step into my office, please," referring to our small bathroom downstairs. We step into the bathroom, close the door, and sequester ourselves for a few minutes to consider our parenting options before moving forward. Honestly, sometimes it helps us save face too, especially when one of us has become emotionally snagged and we are ready to explode in anger or handle the situation unwisely. Once we've agreed upon a plan, we carry the plan out in partnership with one another.

It's very possible you will find times you disagree with the way your spouse is handling a situation with the kids. Whatever you do, you cannot usurp their authority. Share your concern, but not until you are out of earshot of the kids. Kids are master manipulators. Even at a young age, if they sense that one parent will be more lenient, or that their parents are in disagreement, they'll use it to their advantage. They'll work the system any way they can.

If we consistently present a united front, however, we'll decrease their opportunities to divide and conquer. They'll learn that if they go to Mom and then go to Dad, they'll get the same answers. In fact, it behooves a parent to ask, "Have you already talked to Mom/Dad about this?" If you find out that they have, you're only option for a response is, "That answer stands."

The Power of Prayer in a Partnership

Every child needs praying parents. You may pray for your children individually, but your marriage will grow stronger if you'll learn to pray together as a couple. It can be a scary step, especially if prayer is something you've never done together.

If you haven't ever prayed together as a couple except at the dinner table, you can take a baby step by starting to hold hands anytime you pray: at church, at the dinner table, at a funeral or wedding. This establishes an initial spiritual connection.

A next step might be praying at night right after you slip under the covers. Usually this is less intimidating because the lights are out and you might feel a little less on the spot. If you think your spouse would be open to it, but you haven't ever taken the risk, you might reach out to take his or her hand, and say something like, "What would you think about praying for the kids before we go to sleep?" Praying for each child together, by name, is a powerful intimacy builder in marriage.

Prayer is an important part of seeking wisdom in parenting decisions. When you are ready to ground your child for the rest of their life, it's probably time to hit your knees. When Mark and I step into our "office," there have been many times we had to admit that we really didn't know what to do. That's when we say, "We've got to pray" to ask God for wisdom and direction. God has never let us down—sometimes we get direction while we are praying. Sometimes it comes a few hours or days later; however, it always comes! Proverbs 24:3-4 captures that promise: "By wisdom a house is built, and through understanding it is established; through knowledge its rooms are filled with rare and beautiful treasures."

A Managing Partnership

Kids need a mom and a dad in their lives. If Mom and Dad are divorced, the more they can still have a managing partnership, the better it is for the kids. At the very least and for your child's sake, speak only kindly of the other parent in his or her absence. If Dad is completely absent, a father figure is important, if at all possible. It might be a grandfather, "adopted" older man, or even a man at church who can mentor your child as a father would a son. If Mom is absent, a mother figure in your child's life is very important too.

It's also important to realize that even though Mom and Dad are managing partners, they also need their own interests and friendships as well. Dad needs time to pursue his interests and some positive male friendships, and Mom needs time to pursue her interests and encouraging female friendships. Recently, my husband took a four-day golf getaway with three friends. In order for him to be able to do that, I had to be his teammate and handle things in his absence. I also had to be his cheerleader to encourage him to pursue his favorite activity with his friends.

When Mom and Dad pursue a managing partnership, they provide vision, leadership, and guidance to their children. Their strong alliance is a firm foundation for their family, which will launch their children into adulthood and ultimately prepare them to be parents themselves one day.

When Mom and Dad are managing partners, their hearts are knit together to make their marriage and their home all it can be.

16

Kids, Builders
Under Construction

The illusions of childhood are necessary experiences.
A child should not be denied a balloon because an
adult knows that sooner or later it will burst.

MARCELENE COX

Our daughter Anne and her fiancé, Matt, carefully opened each present at their wedding shower. A set of towels, kitchen utensils, bathroom rugs, a tool set, lawn chairs…all wonderful items to help them start their new life together. They were excited about their upcoming wedding, but also about setting up the apartment they found in the far northern suburb of Chicago where they'll be living.

Both Anne and Matt know that while household items are important in establishing a place to live, those items will not turn that house into a home. It is the relationship skills they have learned and will learn more about that will keep their hearts at home. Up to this point, they have been kids, and then young adults under construction. They have learned about themselves, about the world they live in, and more recently about love and all the joy that brings to our lives.

"Childhood…we get only one pass at it, and yet it dictates the quality of the rest of our lives," says Compassion International CEO Wes Stafford. "What we think, feel, experience, and endure in this earliest phase is the single most important indicator of what the rest of life is going to be like."[1] Today's children are the husbands, wives, and parents of tomorrow. They are future home builders under construction. What does a child need to be a successful member of society? What do they need to experience and understand to not only succeed, but flourish in life? I believe we've come full circle now. It all comes down to understanding a child's needs and how home should give them the start in life they need.

A Need to Be Protected

We noticed the nest just a few days after it had been built. The mother bird had chosen one of our hanging flower baskets on the front porch as a home for her family. The eggs appeared sometime during the next week, and we watched that mother bird sit on those eggs most of each day. One day she seemed to be gone for quite some time. We carefully pulled down the flower basket and found three baby birds sound asleep. An accidental jar of the basket, however, woke them up, and they instinctively raised their heads and opened their mouths to ready themselves for food they thought their mother was bringing to them.

Those baby birds are very much like our children, and our home is like that nest. Children need a place where they are safe and protected until they are able to fly on their own. Initially, a baby is helpless and needs all of its physical and emotional needs met. This is when bonding and attachment take place, especially during the first 18 months of life.

Over time a child begins to leave the nest occasionally for school, church, and other activities, but they are only able to do so because they know they can come home. Home is their safe place—it's the one constant in their life. In *A Mother's Touch,* Elise Arndt echoes this when she says, "Keep your baby birds close to you—the closer the better. God will give you the ability and grace to cope. All too soon your babies will fly out of the nest, and you will be proud that you have had a vital part in the formation of their character."[2]

A child has a need to be protected while they are preparing to someday leave the nest. It is at home that they feel the safety of family relationships where they can learn about respect, grace, and forgiveness. It is here that they learn how to live with other people, how to trust, and how to be trustworthy. *That's the importance of home being a safe house, and providing a child the protection they so desperately need.*

A Need to Rest

I packed a picnic lunch and we headed out for a day at the park. "Are we really spending the whole day at the park, Mom?" my boys asked eagerly. "Yes, we are. We're going to play, read, lay on a blanket, watch the clouds, play some more, eat, and just pull off on the side of the road of life and enjoy a day away." "Wow, this is going to be so much fun!" they exclaimed. And it was! It was fun, relaxing, rejuvenating, refreshing, and oh so restful.

Kids need to be kids, and they need enough margin in their life for large portions of unscheduled time in their days. This helps them maintain balance physically and emotionally.

Each afternoon in the summer we have rest time as a family. Everyone heads to their bedroom and either reads quietly or takes a much-needed nap. It's refueling for each of us, and gives us the personal space we need. Kids don't know they need to just step away from the pace of the day, but they do need it. Eventually they'll outgrow naps during the preschool years and then they'll grow right back into needing them somewhere around age 13 or 14. But even if they're not napping, they still need to know how to pull off the highway of life and find the rest they need. *Now we understand that when home is a rest area, it provides the slower pace and the rest a child very much needs.*

A Need to Be Cared For

Anne and I sat and watched the *Oprah* show in disbelief. The show was about pushy parents and what they will do to make their dreams come true for their children to become sport stars. Once the stories were shared, Oprah began to ask tough questions, such as "Whose dream is this? The child's dream or the parent's dream?"

One dad shared that his nine-year-old son was training to be an NFL football player. He talked about how he allowed his son ten seconds to cry when he gets hurt and then he has to buck up and move on. Oprah really pushed that one and asked why. The father responded that his boy has to keep his head in the game, and if he becomes too emotional about a hurt or a failure, he'll be distracted on the next play. Oprah pushed some more and finally said, "That works great for a football player, but what about for the emotional needs of a nine-year-old boy?" The father paused and said quietly, "I've never thought about that."

As parents we cannot afford to not think about our children's emotional needs. Their emotional development happens within the safety of the family unit. This is where we learn to grieve loss, celebrate victory, and lose gracefully. A child's emotional needs have to be tended and cared for, especially when it feels as though the world is throwing darts in their direction.

Disappointment will happen, failure will be experienced, losses will occur, and inevitably every child will have emotional wounds that need to be cleaned out, bandaged, and cared for until they are fully healed. Children need their family to care for them and they need to be able to cry for more than ten seconds. They need to know they are special to their parents, and that their parents will have time to listen when the child needs to talk. *That's why home needs to function as a trauma unit, where a child finds the emotional care he greatly needs.*

A Need to Know God

When you walk into 15-year-old Erica's bedroom, the pink is overwhelming. Her walls, bedspread, and window coverings are all different shades of pink. It's definitely a feminine room. But once you get past the pink, you begin to notice the index cards posted on the walls. There are dozens of them. Each brightly colored card has a Bible verse written on it in brightly colored marker. This is how Erica has chosen to "wallpaper" her room.

It warms my heart to walk in her room because there was a season of time where I experienced a sense of helplessness when it came to Erica's faith. I remember the day she exclaimed, "I don't know that I believe what you believe! I don't know that I even believe God exists!" My heart pleaded to God in prayer throughout her seventh and eighth grade years, which I now refer to as "Erica's Dark Ages." Little did we know how negatively one particular friend was influencing Erica, especially in her faith journey. She was floundering in her search for solid ground. It had always been there, but this time she had to find it for herself.

In *Too Small to Ignore,* Dr. Wes Stafford implores parents to introduce their children to Jesus Christ: "Research indicates that the vast majority of people who become Christians do so while still children, usually before the age of fourteen. If a person hasn't accepted Christ as a youth, studies tell us that the probability he or she will ever know Jesus is only 23 percent."[3] You and I are the hands and feet of Jesus to our children. Their faith experience in our home will be far more influential than any faith experience they have at church.

We can't be everywhere our children are, but God can. We can't meet their every need, but God can. We can't know what's going on inside their heart, but God does. Introducing them to a relationship with Jesus Christ introduces them to a friend who'll last a lifetime. This is the most precious gift a parent can give a child. *Because of this, our home needs to be a church where a child finds faith that lasts an eternity.*

A Need to Be Celebrated

Several months after we adopted Kolya, he asked about his birthday. Kids at school were having birthday parties, causing him to think about his own special day. We told him his birthday was February 22, but he argued with us that it was February 1. We showed him his birth certificate, but he still argued. Finally, after talking with other adoptive parents from his orphanage, we came to understand that birthdays were celebrated on the first of each month. For his first nine birthdays, he had celebrated his birthday on February 1. Therefore, he thought that was his actual birthday.

February finally rolled around and it was time to celebrate Kolya's tenth birthday. Throughout the month we talked about his upcoming party and answered his questions over and over. "Is this party only for me?" "Will people bring presents and they are only for me?" He couldn't get over the fact that *he* was being celebrated.

Whether it is a birthday or an accomplishment or even acknowledging an effort, a child needs to be celebrated and told how wonderful they are. Words that build up need to be given liberally, and words that correct or chastise need to be given sparingly and carefully. As a parent, it becomes easy to nit-pick at our children. We live with them all the time, and our impatience often leaves little room for grace. We have to be so careful, though, because our words weigh a lot to a child. They long to hear us tell them they have done well, they need us to cheer them on, and they need to know that we celebrate every part of who God made them to be! *This is our reminder that when home is a pep rally, a child's individuality is celebrated and their need for affirmation is met.*

A Need to Explore

"Mom, I think I want to take an art class next year," said Evan, just nearing the end of his freshman year in high school. "What makes you want to do that, Evan? I don't ever remember you drawing or doodling or showing any interest in art," I responded. "I don't know. I just want to try it," he answered.

Evan registered for the art class, even though I thought it was a left field request. Maybe there was a girl registering for the class that he liked. Maybe a friend was begging him to take the class with him. The concept that Evan might have some artistic ability in him never crossed my mind.

As the school year began and Evan started to bring home his art projects, I realized how wrong I was. This boy didn't have *some* ability—he was good. Very good, in fact. His favorite medium proved to be oil painting, and now the walls in our home are graced with some of his best work. Evan needed to explore his talents and research his abilities. Because one of the best times to do that is during the childhood and adolescent years, parents need to understand a child's need to explore. One father, whose son plays baseball, said with a tint of sadness in his voice, "I think I would have been a good baseball player as a kid, but my parents were too busy with the family business to sign me up or get me to practices and games."

As with anything in life, balance in exploring is key. A child can have so many opportunities that they become stressed and overwhelmed. Sometimes parents forget that a child is just that—a child. The father I spoke about earlier on *Oprah* whose nine-year-old son was training to be in the NFL, made a statement that his son was a "young man who wanted to do his best." The psychologist Oprah had on the show corrected the father and said, "Let's get one thing straight. He isn't a young man; he is a child. You have to get that straight in your mind." Our children are children. Even our teenagers are children—not fully developed, still in need of direction, not capable of making it in the world without the care and guidance of a parent. Letting kids explore, while keeping boundaries in place, is one of the greatest needs a child has. *That's why home needs to be a research lab, so a child is free to explore and discover the talents and gifts God has given them.*

A Need to Learn

"Boys, your cousin is leaving now. Let's stop what we're doing and give him a proper send-off," were the instructions I gave to Kolya and Austin. Their cousin Miles had spent five days at our home for a summer vacation visit, and he was now heading back to his Indianapolis home, three hours away. This was a manners lesson in the making. We all headed to the porch, gave hugs, and waved goodbye as Miles drove off with his parents.

Children have so much to learn in the school of life. Some of it is learned by direct instruction and some is learned from the environment in which they live as evidenced by this poem by Dorothy Law Nolte:

CHILDREN LEARN WHAT THEY LIVE
Dorothy Law Nolte

If children live with criticism, they learn to condemn.

If children live with hostility, they learn to fight.

If children live with ridicule, they learn to feel shy.

If children live with shame, they learn to feel guilty.

If children live with encouragement, they learn confidence.

If children live with tolerance, they learn patience.

If children live with praise, they learn appreciation.

If children live with acceptance, they learn to love.

If children live with approval, they learn to like themselves.

If children live with honesty, they learn truthfulness.

If children live with security, they learn to have faith
in themselves and in those about them.

If children live with friendliness, they learn the world
is a nice place in which to live.

A child has a right and a need to learn all they can about the world they live in and the people they live with. They need the freedom to explore and ask questions. More than anything, they need Mom and Dad to be teachers they can respect and trust. *This is why home needs to be a school where children can learn lessons to give them a foundation of learning for life.*

A Need to Know Their Heritage

A strong sense of family identity can do far more for combating peer pressure than any lecture on drugs or alcohol. A child is born

into a family unit with an identity of its own. The people who pre-
ceded them in life have left their thumbprint on the family. And
throughout time, God has been at work, setting the stage for their
life. Our children need to know their heritage. They need to be told
of God's hand at work in their life even before they ever knew about
it. There is even value in knowing the mistakes of the past so they
can better understand the dynamics of the family and places in their
life they'll want to make different choices.

Eventually we all make the transition from knowing our heritage to leaving a legacy ourselves. The decisions we make today
will someday impact the lives of our grandchildren and their children. *Thus we understand a child's need to know their heritage, because
someday it will be theirs to pass on to generations to come.*

A Need to Play

I'd never heard so much giggling in my life. There was laughter
and shrieks of delight coming from our yard. When I got to the
window I saw what all the commotion was about. The boys had
hooked up the sprinkler and placed it under the trampoline. They
were taking turns jumping on the trampoline in the spraying
water.

Play is a child's work. They need to play hard, laugh, and have a
good time. They need to be bored and figure out how to entertain
themselves. They need to use their imagination and pretend for
hours on end.

Kids also benefit from the family playing together. They need
to see Mom and Dad move out of their "serious parent" role to
laugh, play, and have fun. This increases family intimacy, fosters
communication, and deepens relationships. It also sets the tempo
for generations to come. Kids who have playful parents will more
likely become playful parents themselves. Says Wes Stafford, "Your
small pebble in the pond of one child's life may send out ripples
that eventually transform many others."[4] We are sending ripples of
influence into generations to come.

Too many children hear their parents say the word "tomorrow," but tomorrow never comes. "Tomorrow I'll play ball with you." "Tomorrow we can play Monopoly." "Tomorrow I'll take you to the park." Of course, tomorrow brings its own challenges and playing ball, Monopoly, or visiting the park aren't the priority then, either.

Kids need parents to make play a priority because it is an important part of a child's life. When we see our children's request to play as an interruption to our to-do list, we'll never make play a priority. However, when we see their request as something that is on our to-do list, we'll have no trouble making it happen. *That's why home needs to be a playground, where a child's need to play and delight in life can be experienced to its fullest.*

A Need to Organize and Manage Their Personal Life

From the time children enter school, there is a blended effort between home and school to train them to take care of their personal property and be responsible for their schoolwork. In preschool, it begins with managing their backpack (hanging it up, putting homework in it, giving graded papers to Mom, etc.). During grade school, the responsibilities increase to managing a desk and/or locker and being responsible to complete and turn in homework assignments on time. In junior high and high school, they are required to manage their time, set priorities, and learn to pace themselves as they begin to balance homework, extracurricular activities, and maybe even a part-time job. They also need basic organizational skills to keep notes organized and research for papers in order. By the time they head into college, trade school, or their first job, they need to have a firm grasp of time and paper management. Realistically, there are many college students still learning these lessons, but our goal is to give our children more and more responsibilities in managing their own personal life.

Once adulthood is reached, the world requires us to organize and manage responsibly. If we don't, the consequences of late fees, bad credit, or not being able to return an item because we can't find the receipt will demand that good organizational processes are in place. *This is why home needs to be a business office, so organizational and self-management skills are established for a lifetime.*

A Need to Give

"Kids, let me tell you about dinner tonight. We're having two guests for dinner: a single mom and her two-year-old son. I want you to make them feel welcome, and I want each of you to spend some time playing with the little boy. That will be good for you, and it will be good for the mom, who can benefit from some adult conversation without having to chase a two-year-old around all evening." Thus began some instructions I gave my three younger kids one summer afternoon. Extending a little bit of hospitality helped each of the kids step out of their self-focused mind-sets into an opportunity to be others focused for a short period of time. Because of it, all of us enjoyed a pleasant evening.

Children need to be given opportunity and responsibility to care for the needs of others. They need to know that they have something (time, talent, encouragement, etc.) to offer to others. This is an extension of one of the first lessons any child learns: We need to share.

Sharing requires that we give up something we would like to have. First sharing lessons usually take place in the toddler years with sharing toys with other children. The lessons expand to sharing a parent with a sibling, letting a friend choose the first cookie, and helping with a job around the house. All of these require some sort of sacrifice, which is really at the heart of learning to give.

Developing a generous, benevolent heart in a child is an important goal for a parent. It can only happen when children have the chance to put others' needs before their own. Breaking selfishness in the heart of a child is a challenge, but not an impossibility. The more opportunities they have to consider something larger than their perspective, the quicker they'll develop their gift of hospitality and enlarge their heart to care for others. *This is why home needs to be a hospitality house, so children can learn to give of themselves and let others know they care.*

A Need to Understand Their World

"Mom, did you know there are kids in this world that have never even seen a Bible?" asked Austin one evening after Vacation Bible School. "I have three Bibles and they don't even have one. That just doesn't seem right." After listening to the missions speaker that summer evening, Austin's world seemed to get just a little bit bigger.

Every child needs to understand their world and how they fit into it. When they grasp that many are less fortunate than they are, their gratitude increases. Children need to be intrigued by other people's unique experiences and cultures, allowing them to grow a heart of tolerance and diversity. Exposure to other cultural experiences helps tame a child's fears by making differences less intimidating.

When a child can see that God has created each person uniquely, he begins to understand his Creator more. When he understands God better, he becomes more effective at sharing his faith with those who don't know Him. *Thus we understand the importance of home being a cultural center so that a child can appreciate the diverse world in which we live.*

A Need to Follow

"Mom, that was neat when you told Dad you were sorry yesterday and asked him to forgive you," said Anne as we were driving to piano lessons one afternoon. She had overheard a phone conversation I had with Mark the day before, even though I wasn't aware she was anywhere within earshot. With children, more is caught than taught. They're watching even when we don't realize we can be seen. Kids imitate Mom and Dad from an early age and, unfortunately, they pick it all up—the good and the bad.

One day I heard four-year-old Anne scolding one of her dolls. Conviction came upon my heart as I realized that the tone of voice she was using was a direct imitation of me. Oh, I'd never "taught" her to talk like that—but I'd modeled it for her one too many times when I was irritable and impatient. Anne simply followed my lead. This time I led her astray.

It was Charles Spurgeon who said, "Train your child in the way in which you should have gone yourself." As parents, we'll all make mistakes. However, we might be better leaders for our children if we will remember their innate need to follow. A child is somewhat of a blank slate when they come into this world. They may be hard-wired, but the software isn't installed yet. We're the ones who have the opportunity to choose what programs we'll install in their hearts and minds. It's important that we program with intentionality rather than allowing cultural default to determine what they learn.

Because a child needs to learn, they have to respect their teacher. When Mom and Dad are managing partners, establishing authority in their child's life is one of the first things they need to do. A child yearns to follow, but their human nature also wants to lead and call the shots. It's important that a parent give the child clear instructions to follow, with accountability if they don't comply. Parenting instructions aren't suggestions you hope the child will grasp; they are directions you expect them to follow. Children find great security in knowing Mom and Dad are in charge. They'll resist it initially, but embrace it when it is established in a loving, consistent manner. *Therefore, when Mom and Dad know their roles and are effective managing partners, a child can easily follow their lead.*

A Need to Keep Their Heart at Home

It's been said that children are like wet cement. It takes only a little effort to make an imprint in their lives. Every step a parent takes leaves an impression on their child's delicate heart. It is home where most of the imprinting takes place.

Dr. Kevin Leman, in his book *Home Court Advantage,* declares the importance of home when he writes,

> A sports team gains significant advantage while playing on the home court, where its greatest fans cheer it on and create an energy that can mean the difference between loss and victory. It's the same with your family. A home court advantage comes from seeing home as a place of security, joy, and memories. It means the best part of a kid's life

will come from what happens within the four walls of that blessed place spelled H-O-M-E. It means his or her parents won't let the outside world with all its enticements and opportunities take that child away from the place that matters more than anyplace else.[5]

Home...it is a place that matters more than anyplace else. It sets the foundation for a child's life. It plays so many roles in our lives that we cannot afford to not pay attention to what happens inside its walls. Home, and the family that lives within it, shapes us, forms our character, and launches us into life.

It is because of this truth that my heart is at home.

Discussion Guide

Discussion Guide

Whether you are reading this book on your own or with a group, there is always value to pausing along the way and reflecting on what you've read. Doing so helps us to digest what we've learned and find practical application in our own life.

If you choose to use this book in a moms group of any size, the discussion guide will help guide the conversation you have after you read each chapter. When you use the book in a group setting, you get a double blessing. First you'll be encouraged and challenged by the author, and second you'll have the opportunity to learn from other women who are on the motherhood journey with you.

Whether your group is a small group that meets in your living room, or a larger moms group or MOPS group that meets in a church or community building, the most important aspect of gathering together is intentionally building relationships. That's why we've created this discussion guide for you. Our hope is that it will give you the tools to lead a successful discussion as your group reads this book together. If you don't know where to start, we've given you a template with which to work. If you are an experienced leader, this section can serve to enhance your own ideas.

You'll notice that each chapter has a consistent format for discussion. Each section serves a purpose in relationship building. Let's take a quick look at the four elements in the discussion.

Icebreaker

When a group first gets together each week, it is beneficial to start out with a lighthearted, get-to-know-you-better activity. The icebreaker time is designed to focus everyone in on the group, the people around them, and the topic at hand. It fosters relationships and builds a sense of camaraderie.

You won't want to spend a large amount of time on the icebreaker. Just 10 to 15 minutes is all it takes to pull everyone together and spend some time laughing and sharing together.

After everyone has had the chance to participate in the icebreaker, open your discussion with prayer. Commit your time to the Lord and ask Him to lead your conversation.

Dig Deep

These questions are designed to facilitate discussion. The best groups are not led by leaders who like to hear themselves talk, but rather by leaders who like to hear others talk. This part of the discussion is likely to take anywhere from 20 to 45 minutes.

If you are leading the discussion, you'll want to familiarize yourself ahead of time with the questions. Jot down additional questions you might present to the group. Create a list of items you need to remember to bring to the meeting. Make sure you pray for the women in your group and for God's guidance as you lead the discussion.

During the group's discussion time, your job will be to draw out the women. Inevitably you will have some women who talk easily in a group and others who rarely share. One of your jobs as the leader is to draw out the quieter woman. Don't be afraid to ask her some questions specifically to help her join the discussion. If a group member wants to monopolize conversation, keep the discussion moving by calling on other women immediately when you pose a question. If the group occasionally gets off the subject, simply pull the focus back to the original question posed to get on track again.

Apply

The "Apply" section is designed for personal reflection and then for goal setting. This helps the reader take all the information they have read and determine what one nugget they are going to own. This is the application to daily life that moves us to action. This part of the discussion will take anywhere from 5 to 15 minutes to complete. If you want to hold one another accountable to make the changes God is impressing upon you as you read together, this is where that will happen.

Pray

You can choose to have one person close in prayer or have a group prayer time. Either will work just fine. Depending on a person's understanding and experience with prayer, prayer can be both exciting and intimidating. If the moms in your group are comfortable praying together, take some time at the end of your group to pray together about the things you have learned. As the leader, take the responsibility of closing out the prayer time when the group is finished praying or when the clock requires that you end your time together.

If your group is not comfortable praying together, then close the group in prayer yourself or ask another member of the group who is comfortable praying aloud to do so. The prayer suggestions are simply suggestions. Pray whatever God lays on your heart to pray. There is no right or wrong when it comes to prayer. You simply talk to God as you would talk to a friend.

Assignments and Notes

In some of the chapters you may find an assignment for the next week or notes to help in your planning. These will help you prepare for the next discussion.

You might want to create a "study basket" specifically for keeping items you will need each week. Pens, highlighters, index cards, notebook paper, and your copy of the book would be basic essentials.

When special items are needed for a specific week, just drop them in the basket and you'll be assured to remember them.

It is a core value of Hearts at Home to provide resources and curriculum to moms, moms groups, and moms group leaders. We hope this book provides you the opportunity to interact with other moms who understand what your life is like. Our goal is that this would encourage, equip, and ultimately challenge moms to keep their heart at home.

What Is a Home?

Ask the moms to read the introduction before your first meeting.

The first time your group meets it is for the purpose of getting acquainted. After discussing how your group will operate (refreshments, child care, start time, finish time, calendar schedule, etc.), explain that each week will have one chapter of assigned reading. The discussion will then apply to the assigned chapter and will include an icebreaker question, a few dig deep questions, one or two application questions, and prayer. You might suggest that they also bring a Bible because they may occasionally need it.

Then have each woman share about herself:

- Name, husband's name, years married
- Children's names and ages
- What she does outside of mothering or what she did BK (before kids)
- One thing she's hoping to get out of this group

If you are preparing in advance, you can also contact Hearts at Home at 309-828-MOMS about materials we can send you for each mom in your group. This package includes information about a free online newsletter and a complimentary *Hearts at Home* magazine. It also introduces each mom to the many ways Hearts at Home can encourage her directly.

~ 1 ~

Home as a Safe House

Icebreaker

What room in your house is your favorite room? Why?

Dig Deep

What do you think about the author's explanation of the need for grace in a family? How can we practically learn to see the choice we have (often in a split second!) between exploding in anger or choosing to extend grace?

Thumbs-up or thumbs-down: How are you as a listener? Of the three listening keys the author mentioned, which do you need to work hardest on: Stop, Look, or Listen?

Does your family offer half apologies ("I'm sorry.") or whole apologies ("I'm sorry. Will you please forgive me?" "I forgive you.") Discuss the differences between the two.

Apply

What is one goal you want to set for yourself in making your home more of a safe house?

Pray

Thank God for the home you have. Thank Him that you have a place that protects you from the weather, allows the family to gather, and gives you a place to lay your head at night.

Ask God to help you to begin to recognize moments where home needs to be a safe house. If respect between family members needs to be restored, ask for God's direction and wisdom to make that happen.

Assignment for next week: Have everyone bring one quick meal idea to share with the group.

~ 2 ~

Home as a Rest Area

Icebreaker
Have everyone share their quick meal idea that will contribute to the concept of the family meal the author mentions.

Dig Deep
In the beginning of the Bible we read about how God created the heavens and the earth (Genesis 1:1–2:3). Read Genesis 2:2-3 aloud. What did God model for us in these verses?

Discuss the concept of margin. Have each mom identify which kind of margin she most needs to increase: physical or emotional. What might be a good first step to making that happen?

Discuss what "time away from the every day" means to you. What activities are like pulling off the highway of life to refuel your tank?

Look up Matthew 11:28-29. What promise do those verses hold for us as moms? What burdens are you carrying that God wants to carry for you?

Apply
What is one goal you want to set for yourself in making your home more of a rest area?

Sometime this week, look at Matthew 11:28-29 when you are at home.

Say the verses aloud and personalize them for you. (For example, Come to me, [Jill], and I will give you rest. Take my yoke upon you, [Jill], and learn from me, for I am gentle and humble in heart, and you will find rest for your [soul].) Ask God to show you places where you are carrying the full weight of your burdens. Give those burdens to Him and allow Him to carry them for you.

Pray
Thank God for each member of your family by name.

Ask Him to show you more ways to make home the rest area it needs to be and to help you personally find the rest you need, so that you are able to help your family find the rest they need.

Home as a Trauma Unit

Icebreaker

When you were a child, what was your favorite home in which you lived and why?

Dig Deep

Identify one time when a family member (spouse or children) had a trauma in their life. Give yourself a grade (A, B, C, D—no F grades allowed) on how you:

____ Loved

____ Listened

____ Allowed them to grieve

____ Encouraged hope and healing

Share with the group your lowest grade. Brainstorm with one another what you could do to improve that grade in the future.

Read 1 Corinthians 13:1-7. Have each person pick out one or two words about love in these verses that apply to what needs to happen at home when home is a trauma unit.

Apply

What is one goal you want to set for yourself in making your home more of a trauma unit?

Pray

Thank God for sending His Son. Thank Him for His understanding of disappointment, betrayal, physical pain, and all the other experiences He lived through when He walked on this earth.

Pray for any family member who is going through a trauma right now. Ask for wisdom in knowing how to walk the journey with them. Ask God to increase your compassion and mercy.

If there is any mom in the group going through trauma herself, pray for her together and commit to pray for her throughout the week.

~ 4 ~

Home as a Church

Icebreaker

What posters were on your bedroom wall as a teenager?

Dig Deep

What did you think of the disparity of hours the author mentions between what children spend at church and at home? Who have you considered to be your child's primary influence: the church or the parent? Why?

What did you think about the author's personal story of being in church all of her life but not really having a relationship with God until the age of 19? Discuss the difference between religion and relationship.

On a scale of one to ten, with one being very uncomfortable and ten being very comfortable, rate your comfort level with personal prayer (praying on your own). What about group prayer (praying with other people)? Is that a place you are content with or a place you'd like to grow in?

Apply

What is one goal you want to set for yourself in making your home more of a church?

Pray

Thank God that He desires to have relationship with us. Thank Him for His grace and forgiveness that allows that to happen.

If you said yes to God for the first time while reading this chapter, thank Him for this new season of your life. Ask Him to show you the next steps in your faith journey.

Ask God to show you more ways to make your home a church. Ask Him to help you see teaching moments for your children. Ask Him to also help you identify places in your own life where you need to be spiritually stretched to further allow you to make your home more of a church.

~ 5 ~

Home as a Pep Rally

Icebreaker

As a child, how was your bedroom decorated (colors, themes, etc.)?

Dig Deep

Share two family traditions of celebrating that your family has.

Brainstorm the rites of passage a child goes through from grade school through college. Share with one another which rite of passage your child(ren) are approaching and discuss ideas for celebrating that upcoming passage.

The author asks, "Are you a dream maker or a dream taker?" Which one describes you best? Share a recent time that you responded one way or the other.

Apply

What is one goal you want to set for yourself in making your home more of a pep rally?

Pray

Thank God for being our biggest cheerleader. Give Him praise for being faithful and loving.

Ask God to help you be more aware of a need to celebrate. Ask Him for His eyes to see traits and talents that need to be encouraged and celebrated in your husband and children.

~ 6 ~
Home as a Research Lab

Icebreaker
What interests or hobbies do you have that you pursue or would like to pursue?

Dig Deep
What interests do your children have that you are helping them research?

When you think back to your childhood, was your home a research lab? What are some things you tried but didn't stick with? What are some talents and interests that were developed? If your home wasn't a research lab, what did you have interest in that was never encouraged?

The author talks about the need to be a chameleon parent. How was that concept challenging to you?

Is there something you've wanted to explore yourself? An interest you've never investigated? A talent you've never developed? If so, share some of your dreams with the group.

Apply
What is one goal you want to set for yourself in making your home more of a research lab?

If you need home to be a research lab for yourself and the timing is right to do so, set a goal to take a first step in exploring your interest.

Pray

Thank God for the individuality and interests of each person in your family.

Ask God to show you how to learn to love the things your husband or children love. Ask Him to show you how to be a cheerleader for their varied interests. For any uninvestigated interests of your own, ask God to give you courage to step out and try.

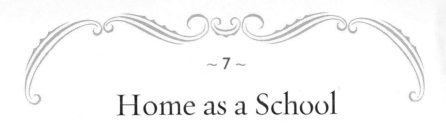

~ 7 ~

Home as a School

Icebreaker
What is one of your favorite memories from grade school, junior high, or high school?

Dig Deep
Discuss the skills the author suggests that we teach. Did you receive instruction on any of those skills when you were growing up, or was it assumed you would just get it? Identify one skill you'd like to teach this week, and brainstorm with the group creative ways to teach the concept.

What home management responsibilities are you doing that your kids need to be doing (laundry, bedding, trash, kitchen, etc.)? If you are comfortable, ask the group to hold you accountable to change that over the next few weeks. Brainstorm ways to make a smooth transition of responsibility to your kids.

Apply
What is one goal you want to set for yourself in making your home more of a school?

Look at the list of character values on pages 94-97. Identify one character quality you'd like to strengthen in your own life. On an index card, write the character trait and its definition. Post the card somewhere you'll see it each day. Take the time to look up the Scripture reference this week too.

Pray
Thank God for being our teacher. Thank Him for the school of life that we learn from each and every day.

Ask God to help you be more conscious of the character trait you'd like to strengthen in yourself. Ask Him to help you be more Christlike when it comes to this trait.

Ask God to help you see opportunities every day to be your child(ren)'s teacher.

8

Home as a Museum

Icebreaker

If you could visit any museum in the world, where would you go? Why?

Dig Deep

What family stories do you remember hearing from your parents?

The author talked about a family history tour she took her family on. Discuss ways you have introduced your children to family history. If you haven't given this much thought, brainstorm ways to begin.

Read Joshua 4:2-7. What God stories does your family have? What could you display to represent that story?

Apply

What is one goal you want to set for yourself in making your home more of a museum?

Pray

Give God the adoration He deserves for being our Provider, for being faithful, and for being our firm foundation in a constantly changing life. (I praise You, God, because You are our Provider...You are faithful, holy, a firm foundation...)

Thank God for your heritage even if it less than wonderful. Thank Him for the life He has given you and the legacy you get the opportunity to pass on.

Ask Him to help you see ways to make your home more of a museum this week. Ask for creativity in displaying "memorials" for your family.

9

Home as a Playground

Icebreaker

When you hear the word "family fun," what do you think of doing?

Dig Deep

Discuss this statement: "Your ability to have fun is in direct proportion to your ability to stand a mess." Do you agree or disagree? Why?

List three ways you can incorporate fun into your family's life this week. Share your list and help each other think of ways to make the fun happen.

Does selfishness ever keep us from having fun? What about a to-do list? What else keeps home from being the playground it needs to be?

Apply

What is one goal you want to set for yourself in making your home more of a playground?

Pray

Thank God for the gift of laughter. Thank Him for the joy He gives us in our heart, even when our circumstances want to pull us down.

Ask God to help you better understand the importance of laughter and joy in your family. If there is anything that hinders you from making home a playground, ask Him to help you shift your perspective to give fun its proper place in your home.

~ 10 ~
Home as a Business Office

Icebreaker

Pull three items out of your purse and explain how they describe you.

Dig Deep

Have you ever "found" money for your family by running an efficient home office? In what ways are you the home manager?

Do you have any methods you use for organization or managing paper other than what the author suggested? How about for your kids' school papers? Keepsakes? Clothing that needs to be passed on?

What calendar system works well for your family? Why?

Apply

What is one goal you want to set for yourself in making your home more of a well-functioning business office?

Pray

Thank God for the "things" you have to keep organized. Thank Him for all the opportunities you have that require you to keep it all straight with a calendar.

If you feel overwhelmed with some of the areas of your home you'd like to have better organized, ask God to show you how to tackle them one step at a time. Ask Him for creativity to develop systems that work for you.

Home as a Hospitality House

Icebreaker

If you could choose your own birthday gift, what would you choose?

Dig Deep

Think back to your childhood. Was your home a hospitality house? How does that affect you today?

Discuss the concept of making your home a hangout home. What does that mean for the season of mothering you are currently in?

Have you ever stayed in someone's home who has the gift of hospitality? What are the little things they did for you to make you feel welcome?

Apply

What is one goal you want to set for yourself in making your home more of a hospitality house?

Pray

Thank God for the home you have. Ask Him to show you how you can share it more intentionally.

Ask Him to help you see opportunities to extend hospitality outside your home. Ask Him to show you if selfishness, fear, or any other struggles might actually keep you from being hospitable. Ask God to help you think of your home as a hospitality house.

~ 12 ~

Home as a Cultural Center

Icebreaker

If you could redecorate any room in your house, which room would it be? How would you redecorate it?

Dig Deep

Do you have a cultural heritage you want to pass along to your children? If so, what is it and how are you currently making your home a cultural center?

Brainstorm ways you can introduce your children to the world around them. Are there mission opportunities through church or child-sponsorship programs you have used to open up your child's world?*

How can you give your children opportunity to be with people who are different than they are right in your own community?

Apply

What is one goal you want to set for yourself in making your home more of a cultural center?

Pray

Thank God for the diversity He has created in the world.

---

* Author's Note: Hearts at Home partners with Compassion International to help families connect to children around the world who need sponsorship. You can find more information at www.hearts-at-home.org.

Confess to Him any prejudices you have held against someone who is different than you. Ask for and accept His forgiveness.

Ask God to show you how you can make your home more of a cultural center for your family.

13

Mom, Site Manager

Icebreaker

What surprised you about motherhood?

Dig Deep

Identify the benefits you experience by thinking about motherhood as a profession. How can you answer the "What do you do?" question other than "Oh, I'm just a mom." Think of answers that will bring value to motherhood in your mind and in the mind of the person who asked the question.

What is the difference between housekeeping and homemaking? Why is it important for us to recognize the difference?

Discuss the need for a mom to find time off. How can you help one another find a break on a regular basis?

Discuss the power of mother love in your own life. How has your experience of being mothered affected you and your mothering?

Apply

Set up a time for your group to do something fun next week (see a movie, go out to dinner, meet for pie and coffee, etc.).

Identify one or two specific ways you might approach your job as wife and mother this week if you really consider what you are doing as a valid profession.

Pray

Pray for the woman on your right this week. Pray for her as a wife and a mother. Pray for any specific needs she has made known throughout the study.

Thank God for the experience of being a mother. Thank Him for the joys of dandelion bouquets and peanut butter and jelly kisses. Ask God for a change in perspective if you have never seen motherhood as the profession it is. Ask Him for fresh vision and renewed energy as a mom.

14

Dad, General Contractor

Icebreaker

Share three of your husband's best qualities. If you are a single mother, share three qualities you would look for in a future mate.

Dig Deep

Does the term "site manager" describe your role and "general contractor" accurately describe your husband's role? Why or why not?

In what ways do you struggle letting Dad be Dad? Is it okay that his ways are different than your ways? How do your children benefit from having both of you in their lives?

The author mentions eight needs that a dad has. Of those eight needs, choose two you need to focus on for the next week. Share your two with the group and discuss practical ways you can meet those needs.

Apply

This week, tell your husband how much you appreciate his three best qualities. You can share that with him verbally (give him a big hug and say, "Do you know what I appreciate about you?") or in a card or a letter.

Write the eight needs that every dad has on an index card (pages 172-173). Place the card somewhere you will see it regularly and be reminded of the needs your husband has.

Pray
Thank God for being the Father we all need. Thank Him for being the perfect parent for us.

Thank God for the father your children have. Pray for specific needs in his life.

Ask God to show you ways to meet your husband's needs, build him up, and encourage him on a daily basis.

Assignment
Bring your wedding pictures next week.

SPECIAL NOTE FOR GROUPS WITH SINGLE MOMS: The next chapter is about marriage, but the principles shared in the chapter are foundational principles in any relationship. Read for knowledge and to gain perspective, even if it doesn't apply directly to your situation right now.

15

Mom and Dad, Managing Partners

Icebreaker

Have everyone share their wedding pictures. Briefly share how you and your husband met while sharing your pictures.

Dig Deep

Ask the group to describe the difference between a family that is marriage centered and one that is child centered. Which term most accurately describes your family? Talk about ways to become more marriage centered.

The author states that Mom and Dad have to present a united front when dealing with parenting issues. Share ways that you and your husband have successfully blended your differences on a parenting issue into a united front.

The author talks about daily dates, weekly dates, and annual getaways. Which of those do you do well? Which do you need to give more time and thought to?

Apply

Practice a daily date each day (see page 177) during the next week.

Set a goal to spend time with your husband. Plan your next date or overnight getaway. You might even want to surprise your husband by kidnapping him for a spontaneous date or overnight.

Pray

Thank God for marriage and the partnership it brings in raising a family.

Pray specifically for any hurting marriages in the group. Pray for healing and help to get the marriage back on track. Pray for hope to replace any sense of hopelessness.

Ask God to help you keep your marriage a priority in the midst of your mothering. Ask Him to grow your relationship deeper and more intimate every day.

~ 16 ~

Kids, Builders Under Construction

Icebreaker

What has been the most valuable thing you've learned from this book?

Dig Deep

Discuss the quote on page 197 by Wes Stafford, "Childhood…we get only one pass at it, and yet it dictates the quality of the rest of our lives. What we think, feel, experience, and endure in this earliest phase is the single most important indicator of what the rest of life is going to be like." Do you agree with that? Why or why not?

Of all the needs a child has, is there any need you can identify that you didn't have met as a child? In what way have you grieved that loss in your life or explored how it might still affect you today?

Can we ever be re-parented? Share strategies on how that might happen (professional counseling, mentoring, reading books, etc.).

Have you ever really considered all the needs a child has? How has understanding this changed your perspective on your role as a mom and being a homemaker (one who makes a home)?

Apply

With paper in hand, go through the discussion guide for chapters 1 through 12 and make a list of the goals you made in the "Apply" part of the discussion (there should be one for each chapter).

Place that list somewhere where you will see it on a regular basis (in your Bible, on the refrigerator, on the bathroom mirror, etc.) and be reminded of what you learned about home and desired to create for your family.

Pray

Thank God for this study. Thank Him for the women you have grown to know over the past weeks and months.

Ask Him to keep this vision fresh in your mind. Ask Him to remind you of all the valuable roles home plays in your family's life.

Most importantly, ask Him to help you remember your value as a mom and the importance of keeping your heart at home.

Notes

Chapter One: Home as a Safe House

1. Todd Cartmell, *Keep the Siblings, Lose the Rivalry* (Grand Rapids, MI: Zondervan Publishing Company, 2003), pp. 19-20.

2. Kevin Leman, *Home Court Advantage* (Wheaton, IL: Tyndale House Publishers, 2005), p. 106.

Chapter Two: Home as a Rest Area

1. Mary Steinke, "The Hurried Family," *Bloomington (IL) Pantagraph,* August 5, 1997, Section D, p. 3.

2. Alvin Rosenfeld and Nicole Wise, "Let Kids Be Kids: Avoiding the Hyper-Parenting Trap," *Primary Psychiatry,* August 2001.

3. Ibid.

4. Richard Swenson, *Margin* (Colorado Springs, CO: NavPress Publishers, 1999), p. 125.

5. Ibid., p. 142.

6. Allie Pleiter, *Becoming a Chief Home Officer* (Grand Rapids, MI: Zondervan Publishing Company, 2002), p. 49.

7. Kate Arthur, "Sit for a Spell," *Bloomington (IL) Pantagraph,* April 29, 2006, Section D, pp. 1-2.

Chapter Three: Home as a Trauma Unit

1. Peter Scazzaro, *The Emotionally Healthy Church* (Grand Rapids, MI: Zondervan Publishing House, 2003), pp. 153-54.

Chapter Five: Home as a Pep Rally

1. Holly Schurter, "Hearts at Home" *Bloomington (IL) Pantagraph,* October 21, 1997.

Chapter Seven: Home as a School

1. Jill Savage and Pam Farrel, *Got Teens?* (Eugene, OR: Harvest House Publishers, 2005), p. 15.

2. This list was taken from a series of booklets by Ron and Rebekah Coriell entitled "The Character Builders" (published by the Association of Christian Schools International). Used by permission.

Chapter Nine: Home as a Playground

1. Jill Savage, *Professionalizing Motherhood* (Grand Rapids, MI: Zondervan Publishing, 2001), p. 175.

Chapter Eleven: Home as a Hospitality House

1. Karen Ehman, *A Life That Says Welcome* (Grand Rapids, MI: Baker Books, 2006), p. 18.

Chapter Thirteen: Mom, Site Manager

1. Savage, *Professionalizing Motherhood,* p. 22.

Chapter Fourteen: Dad, General Contractor

1. Adapted from www.kidsndad.com

2. Ibid.

3. Mary Steinke, "Let Dad Be Dad," *Bloomington (IL) Pantagraph,* June 14, 2003.

4. Willard Harley, *His Needs, Her Needs* (Grand Rapids, MI: Revell Publishers, 2003), p. 245.

5. Leman, *Home Court Advantage,* p. 139.

Chapter 15: Mom and Dad, Managing Partners

1. Leman, *Home Court Advantage,* p. 26.

2. Kendra Smiley, *Be the Parent* (Chicago, IL: Moody Publishers, 2006), p. 18.

Chapter 16: Kids, Builders Under Construction

1. Wes Stafford, *Too Small to Ignore* (Colorado Springs, CO: WaterBrook Press, 2005), p. 16.

2. Elise Arndt, *A Mother's Touch* (Wheaton, IL: Victor Books, 1983), p. 19.

3. Stafford, *Too Small to Ignore,* p. 11.

4. Stafford, *Too Small to Ignore,* p. xii.

5. Leman, *Home Court Advantage,* p. 4.

~ Acknowledgments ~

A book is never the work of one person, but rather the combined efforts of many who share the vision of your message. This book is no exception. A special thank-you:

To all of the Hearts at Home staff. You are my friends and co-laborers in ministry. Thank you for your commitment to the profession of motherhood and the value of keeping your heart at home even in the midst of encouraging moms. Thank you for sharing your ideas about the roles that home plays in your life. Your initial ideas help form the template of this book.

To my friends and family who read manuscripts: Becky, Mary, and Mark. Your input and honesty helped me greatly.

To Becky Glenn. Your help with research for this project and for regularly keeping me organized and on top of things is such a gift!

To my sister, Juli, and my friend Amy, who helped with kids, carpooling, and anything else that needed to be done in the midst of book deadlines. To my neighbor and friend Crystal. Your chocolate chip cookies were just what the doctor ordered for late night edits!

To my prayer team: Becky, Julie, Mark M., Denise, Meme, Tonya, "Auntie," Amy, Mom, Dad, and my husband, Mark. Thank you for spending time on your knees for me.

To Bob Hawkins Jr., LaRae Weikert, Carolyn McCready, and all the wonderful staff at Harvest House Publishers for catching the vision of Hearts at Home and partnering with us to encourage moms. Special thanks to Kim Moore, my editor extraordinaire. It was a joy working with all of you!

To Beth Jusino, my literary agent. Thank you for your wisdom, your encouragement, your vision, and your friendship.

To Mary Steinke. Thank you for leading the publishing arm of the Hearts at Home ministry. Your encouragement, honesty, vision, and leadership have made this and other Hearts at Home published resources the best they can be.

To my parents, Duane and Patsy Fleener, and my grandma, Annabelle Chambers. Thank you for your encouragement, support, and for introducing me to all the roles home plays in my life.

To my children: Anne, Evan, Erica, Kolya, Austin, and my new son-in-law, Matt. Thank you for allowing me to share your stories. You make home the place I want to be. I love you all and dedicate this book to each of you and your future families.

To my dear husband, Mark, who is my teammate, my confidante, and my best friend. Thank you for supporting me in this ministry adventure. Thank you for serving as cook, secretary, taxicab driver, and proofreader extraordinaire! I love you!

To Jesus Christ, my Lord and Savior, for loving me, saving me, and equipping me. Thank You, Lord, for Your words, Your truth, and Your direction both in the ministry of Hearts at Home and during this writing project.

Dear Readers,

I hope you have enjoyed this resource designed to encourage you in the profession of motherhood. For more encouragement, check out my website and the Hearts at Home website. I'd love to know how *My Heart's at Home* has encouraged you personally! Drop me a line if you have a chance:

www.jillsavage.org

www.hearts-at-home.org

email: jillannsavage@yahoo.com

May you always keep your heart at home!

Jill

About Hearts at Home

The Hearts at Home organization is committed to meeting the needs of women in the profession of motherhood. Founded in 1993, Hearts at Home offers a variety of resources and events to assist women in their jobs as wives and mothers.

Find out how Hearts at Home can provide you with ongoing education and encouragement in the profession of motherhood. In addition to this book, our resources include the *Hearts at Home* magazine and our Hearts at Home website. Additionally, Hearts at Home events make a great getaway for individuals, moms groups, or for that special friend, sister, or sister-in-law. The regional conferences, attended by more than ten thousand women each year, provide a unique, affordable, and highly encouraging weekend for any mom in any season of motherhood.

Hearts at Home
1509 N. Clinton Blvd.
Bloomington, IL 61701-1813

Phone: (309) 828-MOMS
E-mail: hearts@hearts-at-home.org
Web: www.hearts-at-home.org

Two other great Hearts at Home books from Harvest House Publishers

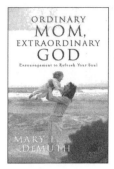

Ordinary Mom, Extraordinary God is a devotional aimed at the deeper issues of the heart and one that will provide a soothing respite amid chaos. Think of it as Oswald Chambers meets Busy Housewife.

Writer, speaker, and stay-at-home mom Mary DeMuth creatively focuses on the gift of motherhood as she considers

- resting quietly in the Lord, even on crazy-busy days
- being thankful for the duties as well as the joys of being a mom
- offering God a heart to prune so that it can continue to bear good fruit

Personal stories integrated with scriptural truth and probing prayers will help you remain connected to the most amazing and extraordinary Parent of all parents.

The Mom I Want to Be: Rising Above Your Past to Give Your Kids a Great Future. Your experience as a mother—and a woman is influenced by the mothering you received as a child. If neglect or inconsistency was part of your upbringing, you need a healthy vision of the wonderful thing motherhood can be.

Suzie Eller gently and compassionately gives you a godly, nurturing model. From her own difficult experience, she reveals how bitterness and anger can be transformed into hope. She walks beside you and shows you...

- how shattered legacies can be put back together
- ways to forgive, let go, and leave your parenting baggage in the past
- how to give your kids the gift of good memories and a great future

With Suzie, you'll celebrate God's healing power...and all that can and will be done in your life as you become the mom you want to be.

Other great Hearts at Home books

Professionalizing Motherhood
Jill Savage

So what do you do? Jill Savage assures women that motherhood is, indeed, a viable and valuable career choice. This rerelease of Hearts at Home's first book includes questions for reflection and a leader's guide.

Is There Really Sex After Kids?
Jill Savage

Having children in the home alters the sexual dynamic between husband and wife. *Is There Really Sex After Kids?* is written by a mom, for moms, and is filled with practical ideas. It is a woman-to-woman discussion—a true insider's look at what works to build intimacy outside the bedroom and improve intimacy inside the bedroom.

Creating the Moms Group You've Been Looking For
Jill Savage

This valuable resource manual provides moms with everything they need to know to start and improve effective moms ministries. This book has three primary purposes: To supply women with the vision and "how-to" of starting a moms group, to serve as a consultation manual for women already in a group who want to know how to take their group or their leadership to the next level, and to provide church leaders with a comprehensive view of a mother's ministry.

Facing Every Mom's Fears
Allie Pleiter

Our world is only getting more frightening. *Facing Every Mom's Fears* shows mothers how to recognize when their fears are out of proportion. With tender humor and encouraging insights, author Allie Pleiter helps women thrive in the paradox of being protector, encourager, and comforter all at the same time. This book is ideal for personal use, group discussions, and mentoring relationships. Questions for personal reflection are included as well as a leader's guide with discussion starters.

Quantity discounts available for all Hearts at Home books—
call 309-828-MOMS for details.